WIRED

(Written In Red Every Day)

50 DAYS WITH JESUS

WIRED
Written In Red Every Day
50 Days with Jesus

Scripture references included in this book are from the King James Version and New King James Version of the Bible.

Books can be ordered through booksellers or by contacting:

Myles Rutherford
1635 Old 41 Hwy NW
Suite 112-210
Kennesaw, GA 30152

Join the devotion conversation. Visit our Facebook page at:
www.facebook.com/3wcdailydevotions.

ISBN-13: 978-0692866290 (Myles Rutherford)
ISBN-10: 0692866299

Introduction

What would happen to us if we ONLY READ the RED for 50 days?

Major parts of the New Testament are written in red. Whenever the words are in red it means those were the words that Jesus actually spoke while He was on this earth. AMAZING!

This devotion does not negate the rest of the Bible but it poses a challenge:

What if we only read the words of Jesus? How would it change our lives? Would we think differently, act differently and change the way we treat others? WHAT COULD POSSIBLY HAPPEN?

Jesus spent 40 days on earth after He was resurrected, sharing His new way of ministry! Then He breathed on the disciples and told them to receive the Spirit. Right before He ascended to heaven, He said to wait! Wait that I will give you something that's going to help you... The Holy Spirit. They spent 10 days waiting...which equals to 50 days.

Join us and take a 50 day journey and get **WIRED!**

Myles Rutherford

Make the commitment to yourself to get WIRED. By signing below, you are committing to:

- Rearrange your schedule and remove any instructions that would keep you from reading daily.

- Spend the next 50 days reading the words of Jesus and letting them transform your life.

- Open your heart and allow the words that Jesus spoke to speak to you on a different level.

- Learn to love like Jesus loved, forgive like Jesus forgave, and have power that Jesus had and so much more.

Signature: _____ Date: _____

TABLE OF CONTENTS

The Gospel of Matthew

Matthew 3
15 But Jesus answered and said to him, "Permit it to be so now, for thus it is fitting for us to fulfill all righteousness." Then he allowed Him.

Matthew 4
4 But He answered and said, "It is written, 'Man shall not live by bread alone, but by every word that proceeds from the mouth of God.'" 7 Jesus said to him, "It is written again, 'You shall not tempt the Lord your God.'" 10 Then Jesus said to him, "Away with you, Satan! For it is written, 'You shall worship the Lord your God, and Him only you shall serve.'"
17 From that time Jesus began to preach and to say, "Repent, for the kingdom of heaven is at hand." 19 Then He said to them, "Follow Me, and I will make you fishers of men."

Matthew 5
3 "Blessed are the poor in spirit, for theirs is the kingdom of heaven. 4 Blessed are those who mourn, for they shall be comforted. 5 Blessed are the meek, for they shall inherit the earth. 6 Blessed are those who hunger and thirst for righteousness, for they shall be filled. 7 Blessed are the merciful, for they shall obtain mercy. 8 Blessed are the pure in heart, for they shall see God. 9 Blessed are the peacemakers, for they shall be called sons of God. 10 Blessed are those who are persecuted for righteousness' sake, For theirs is the kingdom of heaven. 11 Blessed are you when they revile and persecute you, and say all kinds of evil against you falsely for My sake. 12 Rejoice and be exceedingly glad, for great is your reward in heaven, for so they persecuted the prophets who were before you.

Believers Are Salt and Light
13 "You are the salt of the earth; but if the salt loses its flavor, how shall it be seasoned? It is then good for nothing but to be thrown out and trampled underfoot by men. 14 "You are the light of the world. A city that is set on a hill cannot be hidden. 15 Nor do they light a lamp and put it under a basket, but on a lampstand, and it gives light to all who are in the house. 16 Let your light so shine before men, that they may see your good works and glorify your Father in heaven.

Christ Fulfills the Law
17 "Do not think that I came to destroy the Law or the Prophets. I did not come to destroy but to fulfill. 18 For assuredly, I say to you, till heaven and earth pass away, one jot or one tittle will by no means pass from the law till all is fulfilled. 19 Whoever therefore breaks one of the least of these commandments, and teaches men so, shall be called least in the kingdom of heaven; but whoever does and teaches them, he shall be called great in the kingdom of heaven. 20 For I say to you, that unless your righteousness exceeds the righteousness of the scribes and Pharisees, you will by no means enter the kingdom of heaven.

Murder Begins in the Heart
21 "You have heard that it was said to those of old, 'You shall not murder, and whoever murders will be in danger of the judgment.' 22 But I say to you that whoever is angry with his brother without a cause shall be in danger of the judgment. And whoever says to his brother, 'Raca!' shall be in danger of the council. But whoever says, 'You fool!' shall be in danger of hell fire. 23 Therefore if you bring your gift to the altar, and there remember that your brother has something against you, 24 leave your gift there before the altar, and go your way. First be reconciled to your brother, and then come and offer your gift. 25 Agree with your adversary quickly, while you are on the way with him, lest your adversary deliver you to the judge, the judge

hand you over to the officer, and you be thrown into prison. 26 Assuredly, I say to you, you will by no means get out of there till you have paid the last penny.

Adultery in the Heart
27 "You have heard that it was said to those of old, 'You shall not commit adultery.' 28 But I say to you that whoever looks at a woman to lust for her has already committed adultery with her in his heart. 29 If your right eye causes you to sin, pluck it out and cast it from you; for it is more profitable for you that one of your members perish, than for your whole body to be cast into hell. 30 And if your right hand causes you to sin, cut it off and cast it from you; for it is more profitable for you that one of your members perish, than for your whole body to be cast into hell.

Marriage Is Sacred and Binding
31 "Furthermore it has been said, 'Whoever divorces his wife, let him give her a certificate of divorce.' 32 But I say to you that whoever divorces his wife for any reason except sexual immorality causes her to commit adultery; and whoever marries a woman who is divorced commits adultery.

Jesus Forbids Oaths
33 "Again you have heard that it was said to those of old, 'You shall not swear falsely, but shall perform your oaths to the Lord.' 34 But I say to you, do not swear at all: neither by heaven, for it is God's throne; 35 nor by the earth, for it is His footstool; nor by Jerusalem, for it is the city of the great King. 36 Nor shall you swear by your head, because you cannot make one hair white or black. 37 But let your 'Yes' be 'Yes,' and your 'No,' 'No.' For whatever is more than these is from the evil one.

DEVOTION

The Kingdom is Fulfilling

First thing we see in the book of Matthew is Jesus wanted to fulfill righteousness. Matthew 3 is Jesus speaking to John the Baptist and saying, "Let's do this God's way"! Jesus loved pleasing the Father.

I find it amazing that immediately after Jesus was baptized, Satan came in immediately to try to set up his kingdom by perverting the words of God. This happens so often to people who are called and are chosen. We must handle Satan's ways with the word of God. That word is the final authority.

Matthew 5. The first words out of Jesus' mouth are words of blessing and how to walk in blessing. So many times we think that serving God is a to do list and that we are to suffer while on this earth. Suffering means persecution, but true blessing is released from the mouth of Jesus at His first speaking engagement!

Matthew 5:17 says "I didn't come to destroy the law"! His job on earth was to fulfill it. That's our same position…not to live lost or lawless but to live full of love.

Unless your righteousness exceeds: What Jesus is saying here is not that you do more in ceremony but that your righteousness comes from your heart not your head. When you serve God, you WANT to do what is right and not HAVE to do what is right.

Everything in Day 1 has to do with the heart. When your heart is right, maintaining a proper position is easy. Being a man or woman of our word is extremely key in being a believer in Jesus Christ. Anything else, Jesus says "Is from the evil one".

What did the words of Jesus speak to you today?

_____

_____

_____

_____

_____

How can you apply them to your life?

_____

_____

_____

_____

_____

Go the Second Mile

38 "You have heard that it was said, 'An eye for an eye and a tooth for a tooth.' 39 But I tell you not to resist an evil person. But whoever slaps you on your right cheek, turn the other to him also. 40 If anyone wants to sue you and take away your tunic, let him have your cloak also. 41 And whoever compels you to go one mile, go with him two. 42 Give to him who asks you, and from him who wants to borrow from you do not turn away.

Love Your Enemies

43 "You have heard that it was said, 'You shall love your neighbor and hate your enemy.' 44 But I say to you, love your enemies, bless those who curse you, do good to those who hate you, and pray for those who spitefully use you and persecute you, 45 that you may be sons of your Father in heaven; for He makes His sun rise on the evil and on the good, and sends rain on the just and on the unjust. 46 For if you love those who love you, what reward have you? Do not even the tax collectors do the same? 47 And if you greet your brethren only, what do you do more than others? Do not even the tax collectors do so? 48 Therefore you shall be perfect, just as your Father in heaven is perfect.

Matthew 6
Do Good to Please God

1 "Take heed that you do not do your charitable deeds before men, to be seen by them. Otherwise you have no reward from your Father in heaven. 2 Therefore, when you do a charitable deed, do not sound a trumpet before you as the hypocrites do in the synagogues and in the streets, that they may have glory from men. Assuredly, I say to you, they have their reward. 3 But when you do a charitable deed, do not let your left hand know what your right hand is doing, 4 that your charitable deed may be in secret; and your Father who sees in secret will Himself reward you openly.

The Model Prayer

5 "And when you pray, you shall not be like the hypocrites. For they love to pray standing in the synagogues and on the corners of the streets, that they may be seen by men. Assuredly, I say to you, they have their reward. 6 But you, when you pray, go into your room, and when you have shut your door, pray to your Father who is in the secret place; and your Father who sees in secret will reward you openly. 7 And when you pray, do not use vain repetitions as the heathen do. For they think that they will be heard for their many words. 8 "Therefore do not be like them. For your Father knows the things you have need of before you ask Him. 9 In this manner, therefore, pray: Our Father in heaven, Hallowed be Your name. 10 Your kingdom come. Your will be done On earth as it is in heaven. 11 Give us this day our daily bread. 12 And forgive us our debts, As we forgive our debtors. 13 And do not lead us into temptation, But deliver us from the evil one. For Yours is the kingdom and the power and the glory forever. Amen. 14 "For if you forgive men their trespasses, your heavenly Father will also forgive you. 15 But if you do not forgive men their trespasses, neither will your Father forgive your trespasses.

Fasting to Be Seen Only by God

16 "Moreover, when you fast, do not be like the hypocrites, with a sad countenance. For they disfigure their faces that they may appear to men to be fasting. Assuredly, I say to you, they have their reward. 17 But you, when you fast, anoint your head and wash your face, 18 so that you do not appear to men to be fasting, but to your Father who is in the secret place; and your Father who sees in secret will reward you openly.

Lay Up Treasures in Heaven

19 "Do not lay up for yourselves treasures on earth, where moth and rust destroy and where thieves break in and steal; 20 but lay up for yourselves treasures in heaven, where neither moth nor rust destroys and where thieves do not break in and steal. 21 For where your treasure is, there your heart will be also.

The Lamp of the Body

22 "The lamp of the body is the eye. If therefore your eye is good, your whole body will be full of light. 23 But if your eye is bad, your whole body will be full of darkness. If therefore the light that is in you is darkness, how great is that darkness!

You Cannot Serve God and Riches

24 No one can serve two masters; for either he will hate the one and love the other, or else he will be loyal to the one and despise the other. You cannot serve God and mammon.

DEVOTION

Mile marker 2

When I go to the gym I often tell myself I'm going to run 2 miles today on the treadmill! When I get to the 1st mile I look down, only to have to make a choice. Do I want to continue and get the benefits of going 2 miles or is this just good enough right here at 1 mile? I mean come on, 1 mile is really all I see everybody else doing and it seems like that's what everybody else is okay with. And in all actuality, I feel like I've already accomplished something. I bet you can relate to that. When we have the love of Jesus living on the inside of us through the Holy Spirit, it propels us to want to do more than just ordinary. I cannot tell you the feeling that comes over me when I know that I went 2 miles and I made the choice to do so.

Pastor Joseph Morgan, our Covering Pastor, often says "Values determine choices and choices determine destiny". If I don't value someone's life, even if they have mistreated me, wanted to take advantage of me, or hated me; if I don't make myself stronger than their hate, then I have stopped at mile marker 1. I would tell you that doing what is required often gets a paycheck but doing more than what is required gets more than a paycheck...it gets rewards, bonuses, extra!

Today make a decision to do more than what is required in your mind. Make a decision to do what Jesus would want you to do. Today, get WIRED! Go beyond, do more, forgive somebody, let go of resentment, make that phone call today that you have put off, let go of that childhood hurt, just simply do something that will move you from mile marker 1 to mile marker 2!

What did the words of Jesus speak to you today?

_____

_____

_____

_____

_____

How can you apply them to your life?

_____

_____

_____

_____

_____

Matthew 6

Do Not Worry

25 "Therefore I say to you, do not worry about your life, what you will eat or what you will drink; nor about your body, what you will put on. Is not life more than food and the body more than clothing? 26 Look at the birds of the air, for they neither sow nor reap nor gather into barns; yet your heavenly Father feeds them. Are you not of more value than they? 27 Which of you by worrying can add one cubit to his stature?28 "So why do you worry about clothing? Consider the lilies of the field, how they grow: they neither toil nor spin; 29 and yet I say to you that even Solomon in all his glory was not arrayed like one of these. 30 Now if God so clothes the grass of the field, which today is, and tomorrow is thrown into the oven, will He not much more clothe you, O you of little faith?31 "Therefore do not worry, saying, 'What shall we eat?' or 'What shall we drink?' or 'What shall we wear?' 32 For after all these things the Gentiles seek. For your heavenly Father knows that you need all these things. 33 But seek first the kingdom of God and His righteousness, and all these things shall be added to you. 34 Therefore do not worry about tomorrow, for tomorrow will worry about its own things. Sufficient for the day is its own trouble.

Matthew 7
Do Not Judge

1 "Judge not, that you be not judged. 2 For with what judgment you judge, you will be judged; and with the measure you use, it will be measured back to you. 3 And why do you look at the speck in your brother's eye, but do not consider the plank in your own eye? 4 Or how can you say to your brother, 'Let me remove the speck from your eye'; and look, a plank is in your own eye? 5 Hypocrite! First remove the plank from your own eye, and then you will see clearly to remove the speck from your brother's eye.6 "Do not give what is holy to the dogs; nor cast your pearls before swine, lest they trample them under their feet, and turn and tear you in pieces.

Keep Asking, Seeking, Knocking

7 "Ask, and it will be given to you; seek, and you will find; knock, and it will be opened to you. 8 For everyone who asks receives, and he who seeks finds, and to him who knocks it will be opened. 9 Or what man is there among you who, if his son asks for bread, will give him a stone? 10 Or if he asks for a fish, will he give him a serpent? 11 If you then, being evil, know how to give good gifts to your children, how much more will your Father who is in heaven give good things to those who ask Him! 12 Therefore, whatever you want men to do to you, do also to them, for this is the Law and the Prophets.

The Narrow Way

13 "Enter by the narrow gate; for wide is the gate and broad is the way that leads to destruction, and there are many who go in by it. 14 Because narrow is the gate and difficult is the way which leads to life, and there are few who find it.

You Will Know Them by Their Fruits

15 "Beware of false prophets, who come to you in sheep's clothing, but inwardly they are ravenous wolves. 16 You will know them by their fruits. Do men gather grapes from thorn bushes or figs from thistles? 17 Even so, every good tree bears good fruit, but a bad tree bears bad fruit. 18 A good tree cannot bear bad fruit, nor can a bad tree bear good fruit. 19 Every tree that does not bear good fruit is cut down and thrown into the fire.20 Therefore by their fruits you will know them.

I Never Knew You

21 "Not everyone who says to Me, 'Lord, Lord,' shall enter the kingdom of heaven, but he who does the will of My Father in heaven. 22 Many will say to Me in that day, 'Lord, Lord, have we not prophesied in Your name, cast out demons in Your name, and done many wonders in Your name?' 23 And then I will declare to them, 'I never knew you; depart from Me, you who practice lawlessness!'

Build on the Rock

24 "Therefore whoever hears these sayings of Mine, and does them, I will liken him to a wise man who built his house on the rock: 25 and the rain descended, the floods came, and the winds blew and beat on that house; and it did not fall, for it was founded on the rock. 26 "But everyone who hears these sayings of Mine, and does not do them, will be like a foolish man who built his house on the sand: 27 and the rain descended, the floods came, and the winds blew and beat on that house; and it fell. And great was its fall."

DEVOTION

Only God Can Judge Me

There's a big saying around right now, "Only God can judge me".

Most of the time the reason behind that shirt is people are saying don't judge my sin and what I am currently doing. One thing that people need to remember is that the shirt is very correct in what it says. One day, God WILL judge you. He will judge you according to how you lived and did you receive Jesus as your personal savior.

This passage in Matthew does not say we are not to point out somebody else's issue, it says take care of our own first and then we will be able to see "clearly" to remove the speck from our brother's eye. The plank and the speck are closely related. The speck is really a SPLINTER! Have you ever had a splinter? Those things are a pain! If left in the skin long enough it can fester and create infection. The plank is a beam of wood. The connotation here is the beam of wood used to be a splinter. Jesus is saying, how can you help somebody when you have the same thing going on and you never took care of your issue first! So many people want to help people and have good intentions because they've been through the same things, but if that person hasn't received healing for what they have gone through, they can't help! Actually, they end up joining the speck. The person trying to help only identifies with showing the other person their fault. They can recognize the fault so well because they have the same issue. It amazes me how many people pass down family curses because they don't deal with it in themselves first. Today, make it a point to deal with your issues and then you can properly help those around you.

What did the words of Jesus speak to you today?

_____

_____

_____

_____

_____

How can you apply them to your life?

_____

_____

_____

_____

_____

Matthew 8

3 Then Jesus put out His hand and touched him, saying, "I am willing; be cleansed." Immediately his leprosy was cleansed. 4 And Jesus said to him, "See that you tell no one; but go your way, show yourself to the priest, and offer the gift that Moses commanded, as a testimony to them."
7 And Jesus said to him, "I will come and heal him."
10 When Jesus heard it, He marveled, and said to those who followed, "Assuredly, I say to you, I have not found such great faith, not even in Israel! 11 And I say to you that many will come from east and west, and sit down with Abraham, Isaac, and Jacob in the kingdom of heaven. 12 But the sons of the kingdom will be cast out into outer darkness. There will be weeping and gnashing of teeth."
13 Then Jesus said to the centurion, "Go your way; and as you have believed, so let it be done for you." And his servant was healed that same hour.
20 And Jesus said to him, "Foxes have holes and birds of the air have nests, but the Son of Man has nowhere to lay His head." 22 But Jesus said to him, "Follow Me, and let the dead bury their own dead." 26 But He said to them, "Why are you fearful, O you of little faith?" Then He arose and rebuked the winds and the sea, and there was a great calm.

Matthew 9

2 He said to the paralytic, "Son, be of good cheer; your sins are forgiven you."
4 But Jesus, knowing their thoughts, said, "Why do you think evil in your hearts? 5 For which is easier, to say, 'Your sins are forgiven you,' or to say, 'Arise and walk'? 6 But that you may know that the Son of Man has power on earth to forgive sins"—then He said to the paralytic, "Arise, take up your bed, and go to your house."
9 As Jesus passed on from there, He saw a man named Matthew sitting at the tax office. And He said to him, "Follow Me." So he arose and followed Him.
12 When Jesus heard that, He said to them, "Those who are well have no need of a physician, but those who are sick. 13 But go and learn what this means: 'I desire mercy and not sacrifice.' For I did not come to call the righteous, but sinners, to repentance." 15 And Jesus said to them, "Can the friends of the bridegroom mourn as long as the bridegroom is with them? But the days will come when the bridegroom will be taken away from them, and then they will fast. 16 No one puts a piece of unshrunk cloth on an old garment; for the patch pulls away from the garment, and the tear is made worse. 17 Nor do they put new wine into old wineskins, or else the wineskins break, the wine is spilled, and the wineskins are ruined. But they put new wine into new wineskins, and both are preserved." 22 But Jesus turned around, and when He saw her He said, "Be of good cheer, daughter; your faith has made you well." And the woman was made well from that hour. 24 He said to them, "Make room, for the girl is not dead, but sleeping." And they ridiculed Him. 28 And when He had come into the house, the blind men came to Him. And Jesus said to them, "Do you believe that I am able to do this?" 29 Then He touched their eyes, saying, "According to your faith let it be to you." 30 And their eyes were opened. And Jesus sternly warned them, saying, "See that no one knows it." 37 Then He said to His disciples, "The harvest truly is plentiful, but the laborers are few. 38 Therefore pray the Lord of the harvest to send out laborers into His harvest."

Matthew 10

5 These twelve Jesus sent out and commanded them, saying: "Do not go into the way of the Gentiles, and do not enter a city of the Samaritans. 6 But go rather to the lost sheep of the house of Israel. 7 And as you go, preach, saying, 'The kingdom of heaven is at hand.' 8 Heal the sick, cleanse the lepers, raise the dead, cast out demons. Freely you have received, freely give. 9 Provide neither gold nor silver nor copper in your money belts, 10 nor bag for your journey, nor two tunics, nor sandals, nor staffs; for a worker is worthy of his food. 11 "Now whatever city or town you enter, inquire who in it is worthy, and stay there till you go out. 12 And when you go into a household, greet it. 13 If the household is worthy, let your peace come upon it. But if it is not worthy, let your peace return to you. 14 And whoever will not receive you nor hear your words, when you depart from that house or city, shake off the dust from your feet. 15 Assuredly, I say to you, it will be more tolerable for the land of Sodom and Gomorrah in the day of judgment than for that city!

Persecutions Are Coming
16 "Behold, I send you out as sheep in the midst of wolves. Therefore be wise as serpents and harmless as doves. 17 But beware of men, for they will deliver you up to councils and scourge you in their synagogues. 18 You will be brought before governors and kings for My sake, as a testimony to them and to the Gentiles. 19 But when they deliver you up, do not worry about how or what you should speak. For it will be given to you in that hour what you should speak; 20 for it is not you who speak, but the Spirit of your Father who speaks in you. 21 "Now brother will deliver up brother to death, and a father his child; and children will rise up against parents and cause them to be put to death. 22 And you will be hated by all for My name's sake. But he who endures to the end will be saved. 23 When they persecute you in this city, flee to another. For assuredly, I say to you, you will not have gone through the cities of Israel before the Son of Man comes. 24 "A disciple is not above his teacher, nor a servant above his master.
25 It is enough for a disciple that he be like his teacher, and a servant like his master. If they have called the master of the house Beelzebub, how much more will they call those of his household! 26 Therefore do not fear them. For there is nothing covered that will not be revealed, and hidden that will not be known.

DEVOTION

Sonship

Remember you're reading the words of Jesus and some words have been left out to complete the story. To read the full story this devotion should drive you to your personal Bible.

Matthew 9 is probably one of the greatest revelations God ever gave to me personally. A paralytic is lowered down through the roof to where Jesus was. There was no room in the building to get him in to see Jesus. His four friends decided to rip the roof off and get to where Jesus was. There is a lot of good preaching in the story but I want to focus on what Jesus said. When the paralytic was being lowered down Jesus says to him "Son, be of good cheer; your sins are forgiven you". People around Jesus began to think evil in their hearts saying how can this man forgive sins? But God showed me the revelation that it was more about him being restored mentally first. He was paralyzed in the mind more than he was paralyzed in the body!

The first restoration Jesus gave him was the word SON! Jesus restored his position before he restored his paralysis! Wow! I wonder what this young man had gone through in his mind thinking that he was a nobody, given up on and left to just wither away! This is one of the most powerful revelations you could get! You are a SON of God. God talks to sons differently than he talks to servants.

Let Jesus restore your mind today and remove the paralysis and your mental reasoning so that you can't move forward in life! There's no better time than right now to except the fact that God has so much better for you! No matter where people have put you, what you have gone through, nothing can separate you from the fact that Jesus' love towards you makes you a son of God.

What did the words of Jesus speak to you today?

_____

_____

_____

_____

_____

How can you apply them to your life?

_____

_____

_____

_____

Jesus Teaches the Fear of God

27 "Whatever I tell you in the dark, speak in the light; and what you hear in the ear, preach on the housetops. 28 And do not fear those who kill the body but cannot kill the soul. But rather fear Him who is able to destroy both soul and body in hell. 29 Are not two sparrows sold for a copper coin? And not one of them falls to the ground apart from your Father's will. 30 But the very hairs of your head are all numbered. 31 Do not fear therefore; you are of more value than many sparrows.

Confess Christ Before Men

32 "Therefore whoever confesses Me before men, him I will also confess before My Father who is in heaven. 33 But whoever denies Me before men, him I will also deny before My Father who is in heaven.

Christ Brings Division

34 "Do not think that I came to bring peace on earth. I did not come to bring peace but a sword. 35 For I have come to 'set a man against his father, a daughter against her mother, and a daughter-in-law against her mother-in-law'; 36 and 'a man's enemies will be those of his own household.' 37 He who loves father or mother more than Me is not worthy of Me. And he who loves son or daughter more than Me is not worthy of Me. 38 And he who does not take his cross and follow after Me is not worthy of Me. 39 He who finds his life will lose it, and he who loses his life for My sake will find it.

A Cup of Cold Water

40 "He who receives you receives Me, and he who receives Me receives Him who sent Me. 41 He who receives a prophet in the name of a prophet shall receive a prophet's reward. And he who receives a righteous man in the name of a righteous man shall receive a righteous man's reward. 42 And whoever gives one of these little ones only a cup of cold water in the name of a disciple, assuredly, I say to you, he shall by no means lose his reward."

Matthew 11

4 Jesus answered and said to them, "Go and tell John the things which you hear and see: 5 The blind see and the lame walk; the lepers are cleansed and the deaf hear; the dead are raised up and the poor have the gospel preached to them. 6 And blessed is he who is not offended because of Me." 7 As they departed, Jesus began to say to the multitudes concerning John: "What did you go out into the wilderness to see? A reed shaken by the wind? 8 But what did you go out to see? A man clothed in soft garments? Indeed, those who wear soft clothing are in kings' houses. 9 But what did you go out to see? A prophet? Yes, I say to you, and more than a prophet. 10 For this is he of whom it is written:' Behold, I send My messenger before Your face, Who will prepare Your way before You.'11 "Assuredly, I say to you, among those born of women there has not risen one greater than John the Baptist; but he who is least in the kingdom of heaven is greater than he. 12 And from the days of John the Baptist until now the kingdom of heaven suffers violence, and the violent take it by force. 13 For all the prophets and the law prophesied until John. 14 And if you are willing to receive it, he is Elijah who is to come. 15 He who has ears to hear, let him hear! 16 But to what shall I liken this generation? It is like children sitting in the marketplaces and calling to their companions, 17 and saying: 'We played the flute for you, And you did not dance, We mourned to you, And you did not lament.'18 For John came neither eating nor drinking, and they say, 'He has a demon.' 19 The Son of Man came eating and drinking, and they say, 'Look, a glutton and a winebibber, a friend of tax collectors and sinners!' But wisdom is justified by her children." 21 "Woe to you, Chorazin! Woe to you, Bethsaida! For if the mighty works which were done in you had been done in Tyre and Sidon, they would have repented long ago in sackcloth and ashes. 22 But I say to you, it will be more tolerable for Tyre and Sidon in the day of judgment than for you.

23 And you, Capernaum, who are exalted to heaven, will be brought down to Hades; for if the mighty works which were done in you had been done in Sodom, it would have remained until this day. 24 But I say to you that it shall be more tolerable for the land of Sodom in the day of judgment than for you."

Jesus Gives True Rest
25 At that time Jesus answered and said, "I thank You, Father, Lord of heaven and earth, that You have hidden these things from the wise and prudent and have revealed them to babes. 26 Even so, Father, for so it seemed good in Your sight. 27 All things have been delivered to Me by My Father, and no one knows the Son except the Father. Nor does anyone know the Father except the Son, and the one to whom the Son wills to reveal Him. 28 Come to Me, all you who labor and are heavy laden, and I will give you rest. 29 Take My yoke upon you and learn from Me, for I am gentle and lowly in heart, and you will find rest for your souls. 30 For My yoke is easy and My burden is light."

DEVOTION

Negatives Can Turn into Positives!

"Whatever I tell you in the dark, speak in the light; and whatever you hear in the ear, preach on the housetops!"

I used to watch my dad when I was young take pictures! He was very avid about taking pictures of everything! My dad would've been satisfied if they would have created a camera that you could put inside the eye so that he could take 2000 pictures a day! My brothers and I growing up often picked at him because he would hold his pointer finger up and say "Wait a minute, hold that pose". He was trying to capture a moment that could later be used! Don't get me wrong, even though it would be frustrating, later on we would love to see the picture!

He then would go up to a room above the garage. He would spend hours in there. One day I went up there and when I opened the door he said quickly "Shut the door"! So I quickly shut the door. As I walked in the room there were red lights everywhere and trays of water and what smelled like vinegar. I asked him what he was doing and he said that he was developing the pictures that he took.

You see, back before there were iPhones and instant selfies, you had to take pictures and get them developed. Even before there was a 1 Hour Photo place, people would develop their pictures in the dark. I watched my dad take the negatives and put them in water to develop them in the dark. Interesting enough the only light available to develop them correctly in the dark was RED. What is my point? Think about the negatives in your life. You probably think how could God get any glory out of this! But the times of walking in the darkest seasons of your life He is actually soaking you and developing you! The only way that He can develop you is under that red light! THE BLOOD! God can take your negative out of the darkroom after He is finished to show everybody the beautiful picture that He was looking through His eye in the first place when He said, "Wait a minute...Hold that pose"! Every time in your life that you have had to wait was a time that Jesus was taking your picture to make you see you later! That's why He says whatever you hear in the dark, after your dark season is over tell everybody! Testify! Talk about the goodness of God and how He brought you through!

What did the words of Jesus speak to you today?

_____

_____

_____

_____

_____

How can you apply them to your life?

_____

_____

_____

_____

_____

Matthew 12

3 But He said to them, "Have you not read what David did when he was hungry, he and those who were with him: 4 how he entered the house of God and ate the showbread which was not lawful for him to eat, nor for those who were with him, but only for the priests? 5 Or have you not read in the law that on the Sabbath the priests in the temple profane the Sabbath, and are blameless? 6 Yet I say to you that in this place there is One greater than the temple. 7 But if you had known what this means, 'I desire mercy and not sacrifice,' you would not have condemned the guiltless. 8 For the Son of Man is Lord even of the Sabbath."

11 Then He said to them, "What man is there among you who has one sheep, and if it falls into a pit on the Sabbath, will not lay hold of it and lift it out? 12 Of how much more value then is a man than a sheep? Therefore it is lawful to do good on the Sabbath." 13 Then He said to the man, "Stretch out your hand." And he stretched it out, and it was restored as whole as the other. 25 But Jesus knew their thoughts, and said to them: "Every kingdom divided against itself is brought to desolation, and every city or house divided against itself will not stand. 26 If Satan casts out Satan, he is divided against himself. How then will his kingdom stand? 27 And if I cast out demons by Beelzebub, by whom do your sons cast them out? Therefore they shall be your judges. 28 But if I cast out demons by the Spirit of God, surely the kingdom of God has come upon you. 29 Or how can one enter a strong man's house and plunder his goods, unless he first binds the strong man? And then he will plunder his house. 30 He who is not with Me is against Me, and he who does not gather with Me scatters abroad.

The Unpardonable Sin

31 "Therefore I say to you, every sin and blasphemy will be forgiven men, but the blasphemy against the Spirit will not be forgiven men. 32 Anyone who speaks a word against the Son of Man, it will be forgiven him; but whoever speaks against the Holy Spirit, it will not be forgiven him, either in this age or in the age to come.

A Tree Known by Its Fruit

33 "Either make the tree good and its fruit good, or else make the tree bad and its fruit bad; for a tree is known by its fruit. 34 Brood of vipers! How can you, being evil, speak good things? For out of the abundance of the heart the mouth speaks. 35 A good man out of the good treasure of his heart brings forth good things, and an evil man out of the evil treasure brings forth evil things. 36 But I say to you that for every idle word men may speak, they will give account of it in the day of judgment. 37 For by your words you will be justified, and by your words you will be condemned." 39 But He answered and said to them, "An evil and adulterous generation seeks after a sign, and no sign will be given to it except the sign of the prophet Jonah. 40 For as Jonah was three days and three nights in the belly of the great fish, so will the Son of Man be three days and three nights in the heart of the earth. 41 The men of Nineveh will rise up in the judgment with this generation and condemn it, because they repented at the preaching of Jonah; and indeed a greater than Jonah is here. 42 The queen of the South will rise up in the judgment with this generation and condemn it, for she came from the ends of the earth to hear the wisdom of Solomon; and indeed a greater than Solomon is here.

An Unclean Spirit Returns

43 "When an unclean spirit goes out of a man, he goes through dry places, seeking rest, and finds none. 44 Then he says, 'I will return to my house from which I came.' And when he comes, he finds it empty, swept, and put in order. 45 Then he goes and takes with him seven other spirits more wicked than himself, and they enter and dwell there; and the last state of that man is worse than the first. So shall it also be with this wicked generation." 48 But He answered and said to the one who told Him, "Who is My mother and who are My brothers?" 49 And He stretched out His hand toward His disciples and said, "Here are My mother and My brothers! 50 For whoever does the will of My Father in heaven is My brother and sister and mother.

DEVOTION

A Kingdom Divided

Matthew 12 Jesus lays it out! Religious people are calling Him a devil and He answers them quickly. His words are, "Every kingdom divided against itself will not stand".

He actually uses Satan as an example of how powerful the kingdom of God is! He said how can Satan's kingdom stand if I am casting demons out because I'm a demon? Jesus is telling them that even Satan's kingdom is in unity and they don't fuss with each other but you choose to fuss with the Spirit of God casting demons out. He tells the religious crowd not because of what they said but what they "THOUGHT in their hearts". Seems to me because of what He talks about afterwards concerning the unpardonable sin that the religious people revolted against the spirit of God inside of Jesus. Jesus gives them a warning and says you can speak against me, but it will do you no good to speak against The Holy Spirit! You're only fighting yourself!

A kingdom divided currently is religion and relationship. So many people are trying to get to God through religion in keeping with their stained-glass hearts. Many will come to Him on the judgment day and say have we not cast demons out in your name and prophesied in your name and Jesus says some people will receive the words, "Depart from me I never knew you." Those words right there should drive us to our knees and seek out relationship over religion. Just because we go to church, just because we do the routine, just because we watch people worship on the stage, just because we pay our tithe does not mean that we are granted access. We are granted access because of the blood of Jesus as His words and verse 30 of Matthew 12 says "He who is not with me is against me and he who does not gather with me scatters". Let your prayer be today God help me build your kingdom and fall in love with people like you did.

What did the words of Jesus speak to you today?

_____

_____

_____

_____

_____

How can you apply them to your life?

_____

_____

_____

_____

_____

Matthew 13

3 Then He spoke many things to them in parables, saying: "Behold, a sower went out to sow. 4 And as he sowed, some seed fell by the wayside; and the birds came and devoured them. 5 Some fell on stony places, where they did not have much earth; and they immediately sprang up because they had no depth of earth. 6 But when the sun was up they were scorched, and because they had no root they withered away. 7And some fell among thorns, and the thorns sprang up and choked them. 8 But others fell on good ground and yielded a crop: some a hundredfold, some sixty, some thirty. 9 He who has ears to hear, let him hear!"

11 He answered and said to them, "Because it has been given to you to know the mysteries of the kingdom of heaven, but to them it has not been given. 12 For whoever has, to him more will be given, and he will have abundance; but whoever does not have, even what he has will be taken away from him. 13 Therefore I speak to them in parables, because seeing they do not see, and hearing they do not hear, nor do they understand.14 And in them the prophecy of Isaiah is fulfilled, which says: 'Hearing you will hear and shall not understand, And seeing you will see and not perceive;15 For the hearts of this people have grown dull. Their ears are hard of hearing, And their eyes they have closed, Lest they should see with their eyes and hear with their ears,Lest they should understand with their hearts and turn, So that I should heal them.'16 But blessed are your eyes for they see, and your ears for they hear; 17 for assuredly, I say to you that many prophets and righteous men desired to see what you see, and did not see it, and to hear what you hear, and did not hear it.

The Parable of the Sower Explained

18 "Therefore hear the parable of the sower: 19 When anyone hears the word of the kingdom, and does not understand it, then the wicked one comes and snatches away what was sown in his heart. This is he who received seed by the wayside. 20 But he who received the seed on stony places, this is he who hears the word and immediately receives it with joy; 21 yet he has no root in himself, but endures only for a while. For when tribulation or persecution arises because of the word, immediately he stumbles. 22 Now he who received seed among the thorns is he who hears the word, and the cares of this world and the deceitfulness of riches choke the word, and he becomes unfruitful. 23 But he who received seed on the good ground is he who hears the word and understands it, who indeed bears fruit and produces: some a hundredfold, some sixty, some thirty."

The Parable of the Wheat and the Tares

24 Another parable He put forth to them, saying: "The kingdom of heaven is like a man who sowed good seed in his field; 25 but while men slept, his enemy came and sowed tares among the wheat and went his way. 26 But when the grain had sprouted and produced a crop, then the tares also appeared. 27 So the servants of the owner came and said to him, 'Sir, did you not sow good seed in your field? How then does it have tares?'28 He said to them, 'An enemy has done this.' The servants said to him, 'Do you want us then to go and gather them up?' 29 But he said, 'No, lest while you gather up the tares you also uproot the wheat with them. 30 Let both grow together until the harvest, and at the time of harvest I will say to the reapers, "First gather together the tares and bind them in bundles to burn them, but gather the wheat into my barn."'"

The Parable of the Mustard Seed

31 Another parable He put forth to them, saying: "The kingdom of heaven is like a mustard seed, which a man took and sowed in his field, 32 which indeed is the least of all the seeds; but when it is grown it is greater than the herbs and becomes a tree, so that the birds of the air come and nest in its branches."

The Parable of the Leaven

33 Another parable He spoke to them: "The kingdom of heaven is like leaven, which a woman took and hid in three measures[c] of meal till it was all leavened." 37 He answered and said to them: "He who sows the good seed is the Son of Man. 38 The field is the world, the good seeds are the sons of the kingdom, but the tares are the sons of the wicked one. 39 The enemy who sowed them is the devil, the harvest is the end of the age, and the reapers are the angels. 40 Therefore as the tares are gathered and burned in the fire, so it will be at the end of this age. 41 The Son of Man will send out His angels, and they will gather out of His kingdom all things that offend, and those who practice lawlessness, 42 and will cast them into the furnace of fire. There will be wailing and gnashing of teeth. 43 Then the righteous will shine forth as the sun in the kingdom of their Father. He who has ears to hear, let him hear!
The Parable of the Hidden Treasure 44 "Again, the kingdom of heaven is like treasure hidden in a field, which a man found and hid; and for joy over it he goes and sells all that he has and buys that field.

The Parable of the Pearl of Great Price

45 "Again, the kingdom of heaven is like a merchant seeking beautiful pearls, 46 who, when he had found one pearl of great price, went and sold all that he had and bought it.

The Parable of the Dragnet

47 "Again, the kingdom of heaven is like a dragnet that was cast into the sea and gathered some of every kind, 48 which, when it was full, they drew to shore; and they sat down and gathered the good into vessels, but threw the bad away. 49 So it will be at the end of the age. The angels will come forth, separate the wicked from among the just, 50 and cast them into the furnace of fire. There will be wailing and gnashing of teeth." 51 Jesus said to them, "Have you understood all these things?" They said to Him, "Yes, Lord." 52 Then He said to them, "Therefore every scribe instructed concerning the kingdom of heaven is like a householder who brings out of his treasure things new and old."
57 So they were offended at Him. But Jesus said to them, "A prophet is not without honor except in his own country and in his own house."

DEVOTION

Hearing with Your Heart and Not Your Head

Matthew 13:14, "Hearing you will hear and shall not understand, and seeing you will see and not perceive. For the hearts of this people have grown dull".

Jesus is sharing parables with us. A parable is a story that has meanings inside of it. He begins talking to the congregations of people about seed and word and how God works! We find out later in the parable of the sower that in verse 23 those who hear and understand will produce. Have you ever noticed that somebody who has a hard time with their hearing also has a hard time with speech? In other words, when we cannot hear very well in the natural, it is hard for us to speak well. It is the same way in the spirit! When we are dull of hearing we have a hard time speaking in agreement with God! He said they were dull.

Have you ever pulled a knife out of the drawer to cut something as easy as a piece of fruit and the knife was dull? You will spend your energy trying to cut something. What should be really easy becomes difficult because the knife is dull. When our hearts are dull, what should be easy in life becomes difficult. We stress, we anguish, we repeat something that should take only one time to learn or cut through. Jesus says people who can hear with their heart are the ones that will bear fruit. Immediately when the word goes forth to you the enemy snatches the word sown in the heart. That simply means the devil is not after you, he's after the seed that gets in you. What joy it would be if the word of God ever took root in your heart. Salvation is an incredible gift and after that salvation, when you find out what belongs to you, rightfully because of who you are now, you will produce fruit.

What did the words of Jesus speak to you today?

_____

_____

_____

_____

_____

How can you apply them to your life?

_____

_____

_____

_____

_____

Matthew 14

16 But Jesus said to them, "They do not need to go away. You give them something to eat." 18 He said, "Bring them here to Me." 27 But immediately Jesus spoke to them, saying, "Be of good cheer! It is I; do not be afraid."
29 So He said, "Come." And when Peter had come down out of the boat, he walked on the water to go to Jesus.
31 And immediately Jesus stretched out His hand and caught him, and said to him, "O you of little faith, why did you doubt?"

Matthew 15

3 He answered and said to them, "Why do you also transgress the commandment of God because of your tradition? 4 For God commanded, saying, 'Honor your father and your mother'; and, 'He who curses father or mother, let him be put to death.' 5 But you say, 'Whoever says to his father or mother, "Whatever profit you might have received from me is a gift to God"— 6 then he need not honor his father or mother.' Thus you have made the commandment of God of no effect by your tradition. 7 Hypocrites! Well did Isaiah prophesy about you, saying: 8 'These people draw near to Me with their mouth, And honor Me with their lips, but their heart is far from Me. 9 And in vain they worship Me, teaching as doctrines the commandments of men.' " 10 When He had called the multitude to Himself, He said to them, "Hear and understand 11 Not what goes into the mouth defiles a man; but what comes out of the mouth, this defiles a man." 13 But He answered and said, "Every plant which My heavenly Father has not planted will be uprooted. 14 Let them alone. They are blind leaders of the blind. And if the blind leads the blind, both will fall into a ditch." 16 So Jesus said, "Are you also still without understanding? 17 Do you not yet understand that whatever enters the mouth goes into the stomach and is eliminated? 18 But those things which proceed out of the mouth come from the heart, and they defile a man. 19 For out of the heart proceed evil thoughts, murders, adulteries, fornications, thefts, false witness, blasphemies. 20 These are the things which defile a man, but to eat with unwashed hands does not defile a man." 24 But He answered and said, "I was not sent except to the lost sheep of the house of Israel." 26 But He answered and said, "It is not good to take the children's bread and throw it to the little dogs." 28 Then Jesus answered and said to her, "O woman, great is your faith! Let it be to you as you desire." And her daughter was healed from that very hour.
32 Now Jesus called His disciples to Himself and said, "I have compassion on the multitude, because they have now continued with Me three days and have nothing to eat. And I do not want to send them away hungry, lest they faint on the way." 34 Jesus said to them, "How many loaves do you have?"

Matthew 16

2 He answered and said to them, "When it is evening you say, 'It will be fair weather, for the sky is red'; 3 and in the morning, 'It will be foul weather today, for the sky is red and threatening.' Hypocrites! You know how to discern the face of the sky, but you cannot discern the signs of the times. 4 A wicked and adulterous generation seeks after a sign, and no sign shall be given to it except the sign of the prophet Jonah."

And He left them and departed.

6 Then Jesus said to them, "Take heed and beware of the leaven of the Pharisees and the Sadducees." 8 But Jesus, being aware of it, said to them, "O you of little faith, why do you reason among yourselves because you have brought no bread? 9 Do you not yet understand, or remember the five loaves of the five thousand and how many baskets you took up? 10 Nor the seven loaves of the four thousand and how many large baskets you took up? 11 How is it you do not understand that I did not speak to you concerning bread?—but to beware of the leaven of the Pharisees and

Sadducees." 13 When Jesus came into the region of Caesarea Philippi, He asked His disciples, saying, "Who do men say that I, the Son of Man, am?" 15 He said to them, "But who do you say that I am?" 17 Jesus answered and said to him, "Blessed are you, Simon Bar-Jonah, for flesh and blood has not revealed this to you, but My Father who is in heaven. 18 And I also say to you that you are Peter, and on this rock I will build My church, and the gates of Hades shall not prevail against it. 19 And I will give you the keys of the kingdom of heaven, and whatever you bind on earth will be bound in heaven, and whatever you loose on earth will be loosed in heaven." 23 But He turned and said to Peter, "Get behind Me, Satan! You are an offense to Me, for you are not mindful of the things of God, but the things of men."

Take Up the Cross and Follow Him

24 Then Jesus said to His disciples, "If anyone desires to come after Me, let him deny himself, and take up his cross, and follow Me. 25 For whoever desires to save his life will lose it, but whoever loses his life for My sake will find it. 26 For what profit is it to a man if he gains the whole world, and loses his own soul? Or what will a man give in exchange for his soul? 27 For the Son of Man will come in the glory of His Father with His angels, and then He will reward each according to his works. 28 "Assuredly, I say to you, there are some standing here who shall not taste death till they see the Son of Man coming in His kingdom."

<u>DEVOTION</u>

Faith levels

Remember, you're reading the words in red so it may seem like the story is half there. This is for you to have your Bible right beside the scriptures so that you can properly and fully understand. This book is designed for you to have your own devotion instead of reaching for someone else's pre-made devotions.

We want you to direct your attention to Matthew 15:28. He tells the woman she has great faith and then in Matthew 16:8 He tells His disciples they have a little faith. Isn't it amazing that the disciples who have spent so much time with Jesus had the little faith and the woman who needed a miracle and had spent little time actually had great faith? Faith is built by hearing the word of God. It is not built by hanging out with the word of God. There are a lot of professional Christians that know Jesus and will experience His kingdom when they die, however, God wants us to experience His kingdom here on earth! In order to obtain His kingdom, we have to walk in faith. We often say at church that there are three levels of faith: no faith little faith, great faith! Faith is a simple word...BELIEF! Today, decide in your heart that you're going to actually believe the words that Jesus spoke and that in Hebrews 13:8 it says that He is the same yesterday, today and forever. This is exciting! Because what Jesus did for her He can also do for us. His kingdom has NO END!

Pray today! Pray something big that only God can do and stand on the word that He will do it and bring it to pass.

What did the words of Jesus speak to you today?

_____

_____

_____

_____

_____

How can you apply them to your life?

_____

_____

_____

_____

_____

Matthew 17

7 But Jesus came and touched them and said, "Arise, and do not be afraid." 9 Now as they came down from the mountain, Jesus commanded them, saying, "Tell the vision to no one until the Son of Man is risen from the dead."

11 Jesus answered and said to them, "Indeed, Elijah is coming first and will restore all things. 12 But I say to you that Elijah has come already, and they did not know him but did to him whatever they wished. Likewise the Son of Man is also about to suffer at their hands." 17 Then Jesus answered and said, "O faithless and perverse generation, how long shall I be with you? How long shall I bear with you? Bring him here to Me." 20 So Jesus said to them, "Because of your unbelief; for assuredly, I say to you, if you have faith as a mustard seed, you will say to this mountain, 'Move from here to there,' and it will move; and nothing will be impossible for you. 21 However, this kind does not go out except by prayer and fasting." Jesus Again Predicts His Death and Resurrection 22 Now while they were staying in Galilee, Jesus said to them, "The Son of Man is about to be betrayed into the hands of men, 23 and they will kill Him, and the third day He will be raised up." And they were exceedingly sorrowful. 25 He said, "Yes." And when he had come into the house, Jesus anticipated him, saying, "What do you think, Simon? From whom do the kings of the earth take customs or taxes, from their sons or from strangers?" 26 Peter said to Him, "From strangers." Jesus said to him, "Then the sons are free. 27 Nevertheless, lest we offend them, go to the sea, cast in a hook, and take the fish that comes up first. And when you have opened its mouth, you will find a piece of money; take that and give it to them for Me and you."

Matthew 18

2 Then Jesus called a little child to Him, set him in the midst of them, 3 and said, "Assuredly, I say to you, unless you are converted and become as little children, you will by no means enter the kingdom of heaven. 4 Therefore whoever humbles himself as this little child is the greatest in the kingdom of heaven. 5 Whoever receives one little child like this in My name receives Me.

Jesus Warns of Offenses

6 "Whoever causes one of these little ones who believe in Me to sin, it would be better for him if a millstone were hung around his neck, and he were drowned in the depth of the sea. 7 Woe to the world because of offenses! For offenses must come, but woe to that man by whom the offense comes! 8 "If your hand or foot causes you to sin, cut it off and cast it from you. It is better for you to enter into life lame or maimed, rather than having two hands or two feet, to be cast into the everlasting fire. 9 And if your eye causes you to sin, pluck it out and cast it from you. It is better for you to enter into life with one eye, rather than having two eyes, to be cast into hell fire.

The Parable of the Lost Sheep

10 "Take heed that you do not despise one of these little ones, for I say to you that in heaven their angels always see the face of My Father who is in heaven. 11 For the Son of Man has come to save that which was lost. 12 "What do you think? If a man has a hundred sheep, and one of them goes astray, does he not leave the ninety-nine and go to the mountains to seek the one that is straying? 13 And if he should find it, assuredly, I say to you, he rejoices more over that sheep than over the ninety-nine that did not go astray. 14 Even so it is not the will of your Father who is in heaven that one of these little ones should perish.

Dealing with a Sinning Brother

15 "Moreover if your brother sins against you, go and tell him his fault between you and him alone. If he hears you, you have gained your brother. 16 But if he will not hear, take with you one or two more, that 'by the mouth of two or three witnesses every word may be established.' 17 And if he refuses to hear them, tell it to the church. But if he refuses even to hear the church, let him be to you like a heathen and a tax collector. 18 "Assuredly, I say to you, whatever you bind on earth will be bound in heaven, and whatever you loose on earth will be loosed in heaven. 19 "Again I say to you that if two of you agree on earth concerning anything that they ask, it will be done for them by My Father in heaven. 20 For where two or three are gathered together in My name, I am there in the midst of them."

The Parable of the Unforgiving Servant
22 Jesus said to him, "I do not say to you, up to seven times, but up to seventy times seven. 23 Therefore the kingdom of heaven is like a certain king who wanted to settle accounts with his servants. 24 And when he had begun to settle accounts, one was brought to him who owed him ten thousand talents. 25 But as he was not able to pay, his master commanded that he be sold, with his wife and children and all that he had, and that payment be made. 26 The servant therefore fell down before him, saying, 'Master, have patience with me, and I will pay you all.' 27 Then the master of that servant was moved with compassion, released him, and forgave him the debt. 28 "But that servant went out and found one of his fellow servants who owed him a hundred denarii; and he laid hands on him and took him by the throat, saying, 'Pay me what you owe!' 29 So his fellow servant fell down at his feet and begged him, saying, 'Have patience with me, and I will pay you all.' 30 And he would not, but went and threw him into prison till he should pay the debt. 31 So when his fellow servants saw what had been done, they were very grieved, and came and told their master all that had been done. 32 Then his master, after he had called him, said to him, 'You wicked servant! I forgave you all that debt because you begged me. 33 Should you not also have had compassion on your fellow servant, just as I had pity on you?' 34 And his master was angry, and delivered him to the torturers until he should pay all that was due to him. 35 "So My heavenly Father also will do to you if each of you, from his heart, does not forgive his brother his trespasses."

DEVOTION

Heart Splinter

The portion of today's devotion we want you to direct your attention to is Matthew 18. Jesus speaks of offenses and how important it is to not allow unforgiveness to fester.

Just recently I was working with wood that was not smooth. It was jagged, rough and full splinters. I didn't have the proper gloves on to handle these boards, however there was a job that had to be done so we just got to it! A couple of days into it I began to realize my hands were so sore but not from work, from the splinters! I thought I had pulled them all out but there were two inside my left hand that I had overlooked. But one thing about a splinter, you may allow them to be overlooked, but they will come back and let you know they're still there! I noticed my hand had two white bumps around those areas. I had pulled all the other splinters and I did not realize that these were still there. I had to get a sharp object and actually afflict myself. Yes, it hurt! I'm sure you've had a similar experience. The hurt I felt from the cutting actually helped relieve the hurt from the splinters that I knew were going to hurt worse if I didn't deal with them now.

Jesus speaks about forgiveness and how vital it is to our walk with Him. Life is going to throw you splinters, sometimes more! It's not really about other people's actions toward you, it's more about are you going to allow that to get into your heart. Heart splinters are extremely dangerous and have a way of causing infection to set in. You're not going to change the fact that people are going to hurt you, use you, abuse you, and throw you away when they're done with you, but what you can control is your response. We're often singing about the old rugged cross... If it was really old and Jesus' back was laid open from the stripes He had just received at the whipping post, I wonder how many splinters dug into His skin? And yet He was still able to say while He was hung high, "Father, forgive them"!

Search your heart today and look for heart splinters! Get rid of them! They're stopping you not others! Forgiveness is a major key to a long happy and healthy life.

What did the words of Jesus speak to you today?

_____

_____

_____

_____

_____

How can you apply them to your life?

_____

_____

_____

_____

_____

Matthew 19

4 And He answered and said to them, "Have you not read that He who made them at the beginning 'made them male and female,' 5 and said, 'For this reason a man shall leave his father and mother and be joined to his wife, and the two shall become one flesh'? 6 So then, they are no longer two but one flesh. Therefore what God has joined together, let not man separate." 8 He said to them, "Moses, because of the hardness of your hearts, permitted you to divorce your wives, but from the beginning it was not so. 9 And I say to you, whoever divorces his wife, except for sexual immorality, and marries another, commits adultery; and whoever marries her who is divorced commits adultery."

11 But He said to them, "All cannot accept this saying, but only those to whom it has been given: 12 For there are eunuchs who were born thus from their mother's womb, and there are eunuchs who were made eunuchs by men, and there are eunuchs who have made themselves eunuchs for the kingdom of heaven's sake. He who is able to accept it, let him accept it." 14 But Jesus said, "Let the little children come to Me, and do not forbid them; for of such is the kingdom of heaven." 17 So He said to him, "Why do you call Me good? No one is good but One, that is, God. But if you want to enter into life, keep the commandments." 18 He said to Him, "Which ones?" Jesus said, "'You shall not murder,' 'You shall not commit adultery,' 'You shall not steal,' 'You shall not bear false witness,' 19 'Honor your father and your mother,' and, 'You shall love your neighbor as yourself.'" 21 Jesus said to him, "If you want to be perfect, go, sell what you have and give to the poor, and you will have treasure in heaven; and come, follow Me." 23 Then Jesus said to His disciples, "Assuredly, I say to you that it is hard for a rich man to enter the kingdom of heaven. 24 And again I say to you, it is easier for a camel to go through the eye of a needle than for a rich man to enter the kingdom of God." 26 But Jesus looked at them and said to them, "With men this is impossible, but with God all things are possible."

28 So Jesus said to them, "Assuredly I say to you, that in the regeneration, when the Son of Man sits on the throne of His glory, you who have followed Me will also sit on twelve thrones, judging the twelve tribes of Israel. 29 And everyone who has left houses or brothers or sisters or father or mother or wife or children or lands, for My name's sake, shall receive a hundredfold, and inherit eternal life. 30 But many who are first will be last, and the last first.

Matthew 20

1 "For the kingdom of heaven is like a landowner who went out early in the morning to hire laborers for his vineyard. 2 Now when he had agreed with the laborers for a denarius a day, he sent them into his vineyard. 3 And he went out about the third hour and saw others standing idle in the marketplace, 4 and said to them, 'You also go into the vineyard, and whatever is right I will give you.' So they went. 5 Again he went out about the sixth and the ninth hour, and did likewise. 6 And about the eleventh hour he went out and found others standing idle, and said to them, 'Why have you been standing here idle all day?' 7 They said to him, 'Because no one hired us.' He said to them, 'You also go into the vineyard, and whatever is right you will receive.' 8 "So when evening had come, the owner of the vineyard said to his steward, 'Call the laborers and give them their wages, beginning with the last to the first.' 9 And when those came who were hired about the eleventh hour, they each received a denarius. 10 But when the first came, they supposed that they would receive more; and they likewise received each a denarius. 11 And when they had received it, they complained against the landowner, 12 saying, 'These last men have worked only one hour, and you made them equal to us who have borne the burden and the heat of the day.' 13 But he answered one of them and said, 'Friend, I am doing you no wrong. Did you not agree with me for a denarius? 14 Take what is yours and go your way. I wish to give to this last man the same as to you. 15 Is it not lawful for me to do what I wish with my own things? Or is your eye evil because I am good?' 16 So the last will be first, and the first last. For many are called, but few chosen." Jesus a

Third Time Predicts His Death and Resurrection 18 "Behold, we are going up to Jerusalem, and the Son of Man will be betrayed to the chief priests and to the scribes; and they will condemn Him to death, 19 and deliver Him to the Gentiles to mock and to scourge and to crucify. And the third day He will rise again." 21 And He said to her, "What do you wish?" 22 But Jesus answered and said, "You do not know what you ask. Are you able to drink the cup that I am about to drink, and be baptized with the baptism that I am baptized with?" 23 So He said to them, "You will indeed drink My cup, and be baptized with the baptism that I am baptized with; but to sit on My right hand and on My left is not Mine to give, but it is for those for whom it is prepared by My Father." 25 But Jesus called them to Himself and said, "You know that the rulers of the Gentiles lord it over them, and those who are great exercise authority over them. 26 Yet it shall not be so among you; but whoever desires to become great among you, let him be your servant. 27 And whoever desires to be first among you, let him be your slave— 28 just as the Son of Man did not come to be served, but to serve, and to give His life a ransom for many." 32 So Jesus stood still and called them, and said, "What do you want Me to do for you?"

DEVOTION

Marriage and Riches

At the top of Matthew 19 Jesus lays out very clearly what His Father's purpose was for marriage, a male and female and that the man would leave his father and mother and be joined to his wife and the two would become one flesh. This is the pattern for marriage stated by Jesus Himself. However, He also goes on to say that marriage is sacred and binding and should be treated as covenant and not contractual. We are so grateful that Jesus Himself laid out very clearly what marriage is to be. No matter how society defines it, our pattern for marriage is found in the words of Jesus.

I also want to point out in this day that Jesus talks about how hard it is for a rich man to enter the kingdom of God. He says it's like a camel going into the eye of a needle. In our vernacular that seems impossible, but what Jesus is talking about is something completely different. You see, in manners and customs, the eye of the needle is what they called a small door on the outside wall. When the gate was closed, the only way in was through that small opening. It was called the eye of the needle. If you've ever seen a camel that has been loaded down, the only way a camel can get through the eye of the needle is if he is stripped of all that he is carrying and then proceeds to kneel down and crawl through the opening. The lesson learned here from Jesus is not that you can't have riches here on earth, however as you are blessed it is important you stay on your knees and keep yourself stripped from possessions possessing you. Proverbs says to honor the Lord with your possessions. People will tell you and make you feel like because your possessions are more than theirs that you must be special. However, whether you're driving a Mercedes or riding a bicycle, honor the Lord with your possessions. Possessions don't honor God, you honor God with your possessions. The great thing about this is as you honor Him in one level He always promotes you to the next.

What did the words of Jesus speak to you today?

_____

_____

_____

_____

_____

How can you apply them to your life?

_____

_____

_____

_____

_____

Matthew 21

2 saying to them, "Go into the village opposite you, and immediately you will find a donkey tied, and a colt with her. Loose them and bring them to Me. 3 And if anyone says anything to you, you shall say, 'The Lord has need of them,' and immediately he will send them." 13 And He said to them, "It is written, 'My house shall be called a house of prayer,' but you have made it a 'den of thieves.'" 16 and said to Him, "Do You hear what these are saying?" And Jesus said to them, "Yes. Have you never read, 'Out of the mouth of babes and nursing infants You have perfected praise'?" 19 And seeing a fig tree by the road, He came to it and found nothing on it but leaves, and said to it, "Let no fruit grow on you ever again." Immediately the fig tree withered away. 21 So Jesus answered and said to them, "Assuredly, I say to you, if you have faith and do not doubt, you will not only do what was done to the fig tree, but also if you say to this mountain, 'Be removed and be cast into the sea,' it will be done. 22 And whatever things you ask in prayer, believing, you will receive." 24 But Jesus answered and said to them, "I also will ask you one thing, which if you tell Me, I likewise will tell you by what authority I do these things: 25 The baptism of John—where was it from? From heaven or from men?" 27 So they answered Jesus and said, "We do not know." And He said to them, "Neither will I tell you by what authority I do these things.

The Parable of the Two Sons

28 "But what do you think? A man had two sons, and he came to the first and said, 'Son, go, work today in my vineyard.' 29 He answered and said, 'I will not,' but afterward he regretted it and went. 30 Then he came to the second and said likewise. And he answered and said, 'I go, sir,' but he did not go. 31 Which of the two did the will of his father?" They said to Him, "The first." Jesus said to them, "Assuredly, I say to you that tax collectors and harlots enter the kingdom of God before you. 32 For John came to you in the way of righteousness, and you did not believe him; but tax collectors and harlots believed him; and when you saw it, you did not afterward relent and believe him.

The Parable of the Wicked Vinedressers

33 "Hear another parable: There was a certain landowner who planted a vineyard and set a hedge around it, dug a winepress in it and built a tower. And he leased it to vinedressers and went into a far country. 34 Now when vintage-time drew near, he sent his servants to the vinedressers, that they might receive its fruit. 35 And the vinedressers took his servants, beat one, killed one, and stoned another. 36 Again he sent other servants, more than the first, and they did likewise to them. 37 Then last of all he sent his son to them, saying, 'They will respect my son.' 38 But when the vinedressers saw the son, they said among themselves, 'This is the heir. Come, let us kill him and seize his inheritance.' 39 So they took him and cast him out of the vineyard and killed him. 40 "Therefore, when the owner of the vineyard comes, what will he do to those vinedressers?" 42 Jesus said to them, "Have you never read in the Scriptures 'The stone which the builders rejected Has become the chief cornerstone. This was the Lord's doing, And it is marvelous in our eyes'? 43 "Therefore I say to you, the kingdom of God will be taken from you and given to a nation bearing the fruits of it. 44 And whoever falls on this stone will be broken; but on whomever it falls, it will grind him to powder."

Matthew 22

And Jesus answered and spoke to them again by parables and said: 2 "The kingdom of heaven is like a certain king who arranged a marriage for his son, 3 and sent out his servants to call those who were invited to the wedding; and they were not willing to come. 4 Again, he sent out other servants, saying, 'Tell those who are invited, "See, I have prepared my dinner; my oxen and fatted cattle are killed, and all things are ready. Come to the wedding."' 5 But they made light of it and went their ways, one to his own farm, another to his business. *6 And the rest seized his servants, treated them spitefully, and killed them. 7 But when the king heard about it, he was furious. And he sent out his armies, destroyed those murderers, and burned up their city. 8 Then he said to his servants, 'The wedding is ready, but those who were invited were not worthy. 9 Therefore go into the highways, and as many as you find, invite to the wedding.' 10 So those servants went out into the highways and gathered together all whom they found, both bad and good. And the wedding hall was filled with guests.11 "But when the king came in to see the guests, he saw a man there who did not have on a wedding garment. 12 So he said to him, 'Friend, how did you come in here without a wedding garment?' And he was speechless. 13 Then the king said to the servants, 'Bind him hand and foot, take him away, and cast him into outer darkness; there will be weeping and gnashing of teeth.'14 "For many are called, but few are chosen." 18 But Jesus perceived their wickedness, and said, "Why do you test Me, you hypocrites? 19 Show Me the tax money." So they brought Him a denarius. 20 And He said to them, "Whose image and inscription is this?" 21 They said to Him, "Caesar's." And He said to them, "Render therefore to Caesar the things that are Caesar's, and to God the things that are God's." 29 Jesus answered and said to them, "You are mistaken, not knowing the Scriptures nor the power of God. 30 For in the resurrection they neither marry nor are given in marriage, but are like angels of God in heaven. 31 But concerning the resurrection of the dead, have you not read what was spoken to you by God, saying, 32 'I am the God of Abraham, the God of Isaac, and the God of Jacob'? God is not the God of the dead, but of the living." 37 Jesus said to him, "'You shall love the Lord your God with all your heart, with all your soul, and with all your mind.' 38 This is the first and great commandment. 39 And the second is like it: 'You shall love your neighbor as yourself.' 40 On these two commandments hang all the Law and the Prophets." 42 saying, "What do you think about the Christ? Whose Son is He?" They said to Him, "The Son of David." 43 He said to them, "How then does David in the Spirit call Him 'Lord,' saying: 44 'The Lord said to my Lord, "Sit at My right hand, Till I make Your enemies Your footstool"'? 45 If David then calls Him 'Lord,' how is He his Son?"*

DEVOTION

Grace Confronts, Not Condones

So many great things in this one, from the figtree being cursed all the way down to the wedding reception! It's hard to focus on one thing but here we go:

Matthew 22:12. It seems puzzling that Jesus tells His servants to invite everybody from the highways and byways to come to this major wedding hall and great supper but then after everyone is there he kicks one out! That seems almost rude! Here's the analogy:

Jesus is saying that everybody is invited! At the beginning of Matthew 22, the people who actually were on the list didn't want to come and this angered the master who arranged the marriage of his son. So what he did was invited the least, the lost and those who didn't think they would get to come. He invited EVERYBODY. But then somebody shows up with no wedding garment at the great supper. He had not been clothed but he was still partying with everyone. God is talking about people who come to Him and want His blessings but they don't want to change their clothes, or should I say LIFESTYLE. The person was invited but never changed nor did he think he should have changed. He just felt like God should accept him how he is. God always accepts people how they are but when you become a new creation, it should change you. This passage says that the bad and the good were invited, meaning not just the elite but also those who were bad…really bad! However, you cannot use grace to condone your sins. Grace is there to confront your sins and to give you the ability to move forward.

What did the words of Jesus speak to you today?

_____
_____
_____
_____
_____

How can you apply them to your life?

_____
_____
_____
_____
_____

Matthew 23

1 Then Jesus spoke to the multitudes and to His disciples, 2 saying: "The scribes and the Pharisees sit in Moses' seat. 3 Therefore whatever they tell you to observe, that observe and do, but do not do according to their works; for they say, and do not do. 4 For they bind heavy burdens, hard to bear, and lay them on men's shoulders; but they themselves will not move them with one of their fingers. 5 But all their works they do to be seen by men. They make their phylacteries broad and enlarge the borders of their garments. 6 They love the best places at feasts, the best seats in the synagogues, 7 greetings in the marketplaces, and to be called by men, 'Rabbi, Rabbi.' 8 But you, do not be called 'Rabbi'; for One is your Teacher, the Christ, and you are all brethren. 9 Do not call anyone on earth your father; for One is your Father, He who is in heaven. 10 And do not be called teachers; for One is your Teacher, the Christ. 11 But he who is greatest among you shall be your servant. 12 And whoever exalts himself will be humbled, and he who humbles himself will be exalted. 13 "But woe to you, scribes and Pharisees, hypocrites! For you shut up the kingdom of heaven against men; for you neither go in yourselves, nor do you allow those who are entering to go in. 14 Woe to you, scribes and Pharisees, hypocrites! For you devour widows' houses, and for a pretense make long prayers. Therefore you will receive greater condemnation. 15 "Woe to you, scribes and Pharisees, hypocrites! For you travel land and sea to win one proselyte, and when he is won, you make him twice as much a son of hell as yourselves. 16 "Woe to you, blind guides, who say, 'Whoever swears by the temple, it is nothing; but whoever swears by the gold of the temple, he is obliged to perform it.' 17 Fools and blind! For which is greater, the gold or the temple that sanctifies the gold? 18 And, 'Whoever swears by the altar, it is nothing; but whoever swears by the gift that is on it, he is obliged to perform it.' 19 Fools and blind! For which is greater, the gift or the altar that sanctifies the gift? 20 Therefore he who swears by the altar, swears by it and by all things on it. 21 He who swears by the temple, swears by it and by Him who dwells in it. 22 And he who swears by heaven, swears by the throne of God and by Him who sits on it. 23 "Woe to you, scribes and Pharisees, hypocrites! For you pay tithe of mint and anise and cummin, and have neglected the weightier matters of the law: justice and mercy and faith. These you ought to have done, without leaving the others undone. 24 Blind guides, who strain out a gnat and swallow a camel! 25 "Woe to you, scribes and Pharisees, hypocrites! For you cleanse the outside of the cup and dish, but inside they are full of extortion and self-indulgence. 26 Blind Pharisee, first cleanse the inside of the cup and dish, that the outside of them may be clean also. 27 "Woe to you, scribes and Pharisees, hypocrites! For you are like whitewashed tombs which indeed appear beautiful outwardly, but inside are full of dead men's bones and all uncleanness. 28 Even so you also outwardly appear righteous to men, but inside you are full of hypocrisy and lawlessness. 29 "Woe to you, scribes and Pharisees, hypocrites! Because you build the tombs of the prophets and adorn the monuments of the righteous, 30 and say, 'If we had lived in the days of our fathers, we would not have been partakers with them in the blood of the prophets.' 31 "Therefore you are witnesses against yourselves that you are sons of those who murdered the prophets. 32 Fill up, then, the measure of your fathers' guilt. 33 Serpents, brood of vipers! How can you escape the condemnation of hell? 34 Therefore, indeed, I send you prophets, wise men, and scribes: some of them you will kill and crucify, and some of them you will scourge in your synagogues and persecute from city to city, 35 that on you may come all the righteous blood shed on the earth, from the blood of righteous Abel to the blood of Zechariah, son of Berechiah, whom you murdered between the temple and the altar. 36 Assuredly, I say to you, all these things will come upon this generation.

Jesus Laments over Jerusalem

37 "O Jerusalem, Jerusalem, the one who kills the prophets and stones those who are sent to her! How often I wanted to gather your children together, as a hen gathers her chicks under her wings, but you were not willing! 38 See! Your house is left to you desolate; 39 for I say to you, you shall see Me no more till you say, 'Blessed is He who comes in the name of the Lord!'"

DEVOTION

WOE!!!!!

Matthew 22:13, you shut up the kingdom of heaven! Help us God to not be so religious that we block the whole purpose of the gospel of Jesus Christ, which was for us to walk in His kingdom daily. Anyone who teaches you anything or anything you teach anyone outside of this gospel will literally shut a door! The gospel is a gospel of open doors. Have you ever been to the store when the doors are closing? If you're lucky enough, you'll slide underneath the gate right before the door shuts or the gate closes. Think of that store as being the kingdom of heaven! Jesus is saying here that the religious people want you to do it their way without the Messiah! Wow and WOE! Woe means GRIEF! They want you to be on their terms and on their times but God has a big sign on His kingdom of heaven that says 24/7!! The doors are never shut!! The gospel of Jesus is about what He did not what we do in order to keep ourselves in right standing. Let the kingdom of heaven be the store that you wake up in every morning and go to bed in every night. The doors never shut until that one day when the dead in Christ will rise.

What did the words of Jesus speak to you today?

_____
_____
_____
_____
_____

How can you apply them to your life?

_____
_____
_____
_____
_____

Matthew 24

2 And Jesus said to them, "Do you not see all these things? Assuredly, I say to you, not one stone shall be left here upon another, that shall not be thrown down." 4 And Jesus answered and said to them: "Take heed that no one deceives you. 5 For many will come in My name, saying, 'I am the Christ,' and will deceive many. 6 And you will hear of wars and rumors of wars. See that you are not troubled; for all these things must come to pass, but the end is not yet. 7 For nation will rise against nation, and kingdom against kingdom. And there will be famines, pestilences, and earthquakes in various places. 8 All these are the beginning of sorrows. 9 "Then they will deliver you up to tribulation and kill you, and you will be hated by all nations for My name's sake. 10 And then many will be offended, will betray one another, and will hate one another. 11 Then many false prophets will rise up and deceive many. 12 And because lawlessness will abound, the love of many will grow cold. 13 But he who endures to the end shall be saved. 14 And this gospel of the kingdom will be preached in all the world as a witness to all the nations, and then the end will come.

The Great Tribulation

15 "Therefore when you see the 'abomination of desolation,' spoken of by Daniel the prophet, standing in the holy place" (whoever reads, let him understand), 16 "then let those who are in Judea flee to the mountains. 17 Let him who is on the housetop not go down to take anything out of his house. 18 And let him who is in the field not go back to get his clothes. 19 But woe to those who are pregnant and to those who are nursing babies in those days! 20 And pray that your flight may not be in winter or on the Sabbath. 21 For then there will be great tribulation, such as has not been since the beginning of the world until this time, no, nor ever shall be. 22 And unless those days were shortened, no flesh would be saved; but for the elect's sake those days will be shortened. 23 "Then if anyone says to you, 'Look, here is the Christ!' or 'There!' do not believe it. 24 For false christs and false prophets will rise and show great signs and wonders to deceive, if possible, even the elect. 25 See, I have told you beforehand. 26 "Therefore if they say to you, 'Look, He is in the desert!' do not go out; or 'Look, He is in the inner rooms!' do not believe it. 27 For as the lightning comes from the east and flashes to the west, so also will the coming of the Son of Man be. 28 For wherever the carcass is, there the eagles will be gathered together.

The Coming of the Son of Man

29 "Immediately after the tribulation of those days the sun will be darkened, and the moon will not give its light; the stars will fall from heaven, and the powers of the heavens will be shaken. 30 Then the sign of the Son of Man will appear in heaven, and then all the tribes of the earth will mourn, and they will see the Son of Man coming on the clouds of heaven with power and great glory. 31 And He will send His angels with a great sound of a trumpet, and they will gather together His elect from the four winds, from one end of heaven to the other.

The Parable of the Fig Tree

32 "Now learn this parable from the fig tree: When its branch has already become tender and puts forth leaves, you know that summer is near. 33 So you also, when you see all these things, know that it is near—at the doors! 34 Assuredly, I say to you, this generation will by no means pass away till all these things take place. 35 Heaven and earth will pass away, but My words will by no means pass away.

No One Knows the Day or Hour

36 "But of that day and hour no one knows, not even the angels of heaven, but My Father only. 37 But as the days of Noah were, so also will the coming of the Son of Man be. 38 For as in the days before the flood, they were eating and drinking, marrying and giving in marriage, until the day that Noah entered the ark, 39 and did not know until the flood came and took them all away, so also will the coming of the Son of Man be. 40 Then two men will be in the field: one will be taken and the other left. 41 Two women will be grinding at the mill: one will be taken and the other left. 42 Watch therefore, for you do not know what hour your Lord is coming. 43 But know this, that if the master of the house had known what hour the thief would come, he would have watched and not allowed his house to be broken into. 44 Therefore you also be ready, for the Son of Man is coming at an hour you do not expect.

DEVOTION

Ready or Not!

We used to play a game growing up, it was called "hide and seek". A person would count to 10 to give others time to hide, then the person would say, "Ready or not, here I come"! READY OR NOT! Although we are not hiding from God, there is a principle here!

The whole chapter of this devotion is Jesus giving people signs, then He goes about by saying, "Watch and be ready." Notice He's not saying get ready but He is saying BE ready! If you have to get ready you may be like the five foolish virgins who woke up and had to get things prepared and they lost their moment. We believe that Jesus is telling us to MAKE SURE we are always ready! HE IS COMING BACK!

If you look at the signs that He is pointing out, you can find yourself in a generation that may be the one Jesus comes back in. Even the very elect may be deceived! Nations will rise up against each other...nations meaning ethnicities...ethnic cultures fighting each other. White against black, black against white and nations against nations. Sounds like today!?

BE READY - BE READY! What if it was today? Are you ready? On day 13 what if day 14 never came? The point is, make sure your heart is ready and make sure your love for people and love for God is intact!

What did the words of Jesus speak to you today?

_____

_____

_____

_____

_____

How can you apply them to your life?

_____

_____

_____

_____

_____

The Faithful Servant and the Evil Servant

45 "Who then is a faithful and wise servant, whom his master made ruler over his household, to give them food in due season? 46 Blessed is that servant whom his master, when he comes, will find so doing. 47 Assuredly, I say to you that he will make him ruler over all his goods. 48 But if that evil servant says in his heart, 'My master is delaying his coming,' 49 and begins to beat his fellow servants, and to eat and drink with the drunkards, 50 the master of that servant will come on a day when he is not looking for him and at an hour that he is not aware of, 51 and will cut him in two and appoint him his portion with the hypocrites. There shall be weeping and gnashing of teeth.

Matthew 25

1 "Then the kingdom of heaven shall be likened to ten virgins who took their lamps and went out to meet the bridegroom. 2 Now five of them were wise, and five were foolish. 3 those who were foolish took their lamps and took no oil with them, 4 but the wise took oil in their vessels with their lamps. 5 But while the bridegroom was delayed, they all slumbered and slept. 6 "And at midnight a cry was heard: 'Behold, the bridegroom is coming; go out to meet him!' 7 Then all those virgins arose and trimmed their lamps. 8 And the foolish said to the wise, 'Give us some of your oil, for our lamps are going out.' 9 But the wise answered, saying, 'No, lest there should not be enough for us and you; but go rather to those who sell, and buy for yourselves.' 10 And while they went to buy, the bridegroom came, and those who were ready went in with him to the wedding; and the door was shut. 11 "Afterward the other virgins came also, saying, 'Lord, Lord, open to us!' 12 But he answered and said, 'Assuredly, I say to you, I do not know you.' 13 "Watch therefore, for you know neither the day nor the hour in which the Son of Man is coming.

The Parable of the Talents

14 "For the kingdom of heaven is like a man traveling to a far country, who called his own servants and delivered his goods to them. 15 And to one he gave five talents, to another two, and to another one, to each according to his own ability; and immediately he went on a journey. 16 Then he who had received the five talents went and traded with them, and made another five talents. 17 And likewise he who had received two gained two more also. 18 But he who had received one went and dug in the ground, and hid his lord's money. 19 After a long time the lord of those servants came and settled accounts with them. 20 "So he who had received five talents came and brought five other talents, saying, 'Lord, you delivered to me five talents; look, I have gained five more talents besides them.' 21 His lord said to him, 'Well done, good and faithful servant; you were faithful over a few things, I will make you ruler over many things. Enter into the joy of your lord.' 22 He also who had received two talents came and said, 'Lord, you delivered to me two talents; look, I have gained two more talents besides them.' 23 His lord said to him, 'Well done, good and faithful servant; you have been faithful over a few things, I will make you ruler over many things. Enter into the joy of your lord.' 24 "Then he who had received the one talent came and said, 'Lord, I knew you to be a hard man, reaping where you have not sown, and gathering where you have not scattered seed. 25 And I was afraid, and went and hid your talent in the ground. Look, there you have what is yours.' 26 "But his lord answered and said to him, 'You wicked and lazy servant, you knew that I reap where I have not sown, and gather where I have not scattered seed. 27 So you ought to have deposited my money with the bankers, and at my coming I would have received back my own with interest. 28 Therefore take the talent from him, and give it to him who has ten talents. 29 'For to everyone who has, more will be given, and he will have abundance; but from him who does not have, even what he has will be taken away. 30 And cast the unprofitable servant into the outer darkness. There will be weeping and gnashing of teeth.'

DEVOTION

Midnight with No Oil!

Midnight is very important here because it speaks of one day closing and a new day opening. Midnight also denotes that it is a time for some will be sleeping and not watching and waiting. The oil represents the Holy Spirit.

We are living in a day of compromise. We are living in a day that you can go to church and have no oil. It's a day of anesthesia. The church is comfortably numb. Some are at ease thinking it's okay to just do what we want as long as we stay in the party of virgins (church). But you must have oil! YOU CAN'T stay in or condone sin and keep your wicks ready!!

Here is the problem with condoning sin - WE ARE NOT GOING TO HAVE ANY OIL IN OUR LAMPS! At midnight the friends of the Bridegroom are going to go out into the streets and say HERE HE COMES!

We must turn from passivity to power! Turn the lights back on, put fire in the lamps and turn the lights back on! We must be relevant to God and represent Him, not sin. We have to get our own oil. In the last day, you are going to have to get your own oil! Your pastors won't be able to answer for you in that day and you won't be able to go to church to get that answer. You will need to have an assurance in your heart that you are ready. The question is not if, but when will the Groom come. You can own a Bible and not be ready. You can be a friend of church and not be ready. You can have a lamp and not be ready.

What did the words of Jesus speak to you today?

_____

_____

_____

_____

_____

How can you apply them to your life?

_____

_____

_____

_____

_____

The Son of Man Will Judge the Nations

31 "When the Son of Man comes in His glory, and all the holy angels with Him, then He will sit on the throne of His glory. 32 All the nations will be gathered before Him, and He will separate them one from another, as a shepherd divides his sheep from the goats. 33 And He will set the sheep on His right hand, but the goats on the left. 34 Then the King will say to those on His right hand, 'Come, you blessed of My Father, inherit the kingdom prepared for you from the foundation of the world: 35 for I was hungry and you gave Me food; I was thirsty and you gave Me drink; I was a stranger and you took Me in; 36 I was naked and you clothed Me; I was sick and you visited Me; I was in prison and you came to Me.' 37 "Then the righteous will answer Him, saying, 'Lord, when did we see You hungry and feed You, or thirsty and give You drink? 38 When did we see You a stranger and take You in, or naked and clothe You? 39 Or when did we see You sick, or in prison, and come to You?' 40 And the King will answer and say to them, 'Assuredly, I say to you, inasmuch as you did it to one of the least of these My brethren, you did it to Me.' 41 "Then He will also say to those on the left hand, 'Depart from Me, you cursed, into the everlasting fire prepared for the devil and his angels: 42 for I was hungry and you gave Me no food; I was thirsty and you gave Me no drink; 43 I was a stranger and you did not take Me in, naked and you did not clothe Me, sick and in prison and you did not visit Me.' 44 "Then they also will answer Him, saying, 'Lord, when did we see You hungry or thirsty or a stranger or naked or sick or in prison, and did not minister to You?' 45 Then He will answer them, saying, 'Assuredly, I say to you, inasmuch as you did not do it to one of the least of these, you did not do it to Me.' 46 And these will go away into everlasting punishment, but the righteous into eternal life."

Matthew 26

2 "You know that after two days is the Passover, and the Son of Man will be delivered up to be crucified." 10 But when Jesus was aware of it, He said to them, "Why do you trouble the woman? For she has done a good work for Me. 11 For you have the poor with you always, but Me you do not have always. 12 For in pouring this fragrant oil on My body, she did it for My burial. 13 Assuredly, I say to you, wherever this gospel is preached in the whole world, what this woman has done will also be told as a memorial to her." 18 And He said, "Go into the city to a certain man, and say to him, 'The Teacher says, "My time is at hand; I will keep the Passover at your house with My disciples." 21 Now as they were eating, He said, "Assuredly, I say to you, one of you will betray Me." 23 He answered and said, "He who dipped his hand with Me in the dish will betray Me. 24 The Son of Man indeed goes just as it is written of Him, but woe to that man by whom the Son of Man is betrayed! It would have been good for that man if he had not been born." 25 Then Judas, who was betraying Him, answered and said, "Rabbi, is it I?" He said to him, "You have said it." Jesus Institutes the Lord's Supper 26 And as they were eating, Jesus took bread, blessed and broke it, and gave it to the disciples and said, "Take, eat; this is My body." 27 Then He took the cup, and gave thanks, and gave it to them, saying, "Drink from it, all of you. 28 For this is My blood of the new covenant, which is shed for many for the remission of sins. 29 But I say to you, I will not drink of this fruit of the vine from now on until that day when I drink it new with you in My Father's kingdom."

Jesus Predicts Peter's Denial 31 Then Jesus said to them, "All of you will be made to stumble because of Me this night, for it is written: 'I will strike the Shepherd, And the sheep of the flock will be scattered.' 32 But after I have been raised, I will go before you to Galilee." 34 Jesus said to him, "Assuredly, I say to you that this night, before the rooster crows, you will deny Me three times." 36 Then Jesus came with them to a place called Gethsemane, and said to the disciples, "Sit here while I go and pray over there."

38 Then He said to them, "My soul is exceedingly sorrowful, even to death. Stay here and watch with Me." 39 He went a little farther and fell on His face, and prayed, saying, "O My Father, if it is possible, let this cup pass from Me; nevertheless, not as I will, but as You will." 40 Then He came to the disciples and found them sleeping, and said to Peter, "What! Could you not watch with Me one hour? 41 Watch and pray, lest you enter into temptation. The spirit indeed is willing, but the flesh is weak." 42 Again, a second time, He went away and prayed, saying, "O My Father, if this cup cannot pass away from Me unless I drink it, Your will be done." 45 Then He came to His disciples and said to them, "Are you still sleeping and resting? Behold, the hour is at hand, and the Son of Man is being betrayed into the hands of sinners. 46 Rise, let us be going. See, My betrayer is at hand." 50 But Jesus said to him, "Friend, why have you come?" then they came and laid hands on Jesus and took Him. 52 But Jesus said to him, "Put your sword in its place, for all who take the sword will perish by the sword. 53 Or do you think that I cannot now pray to My Father, and He will provide Me with more than twelve legions of angels? 54 How then could the Scriptures be fulfilled, that it must happen thus?" 55 In that hour Jesus said to the multitudes, "Have you come out, as against a robber, with swords and clubs to take Me? I sat daily with you, teaching in the temple, and you did not seize Me. 56 But all this was done that the Scriptures of the prophets might be fulfilled." 64 Jesus said to him, "It is as you said. Nevertheless, I say to you, hereafter you will see the Son of Man sitting at the right hand of the Power, and coming on the clouds of heaven." 65 And Peter remembered the word of Jesus who had said to him, "Before the rooster crows, you will deny Me three times." So he went out and wept bitterly.

DEVOTION

Could You Not Pray with Me?

All through the Bible we see Jesus praying! Here in the garden right before His betrayal, He tells His disciples, "My soul is sorrowful! Stay here and watch with me… or pray with me". His mind was at war with His spirit. Jesus had a glimpse of what was about to happen to Him and His mind was trying to reason with His walk of faith that He would have to have over the next few hours. He comes back a couple of times to see His disciples sleeping and He asks could you not pray with me for one hour!

Today I want you to think of people around you that you see their soul is sorrowful. Could you not pray with them? I truly believe that the Holy Spirit speaks to us about who we are assigned to every day! Yes it's going to be an inconvenience to your schedule, you're going to have to rearrange some things or possibly lose some sleep, but it will be worth it to pray with somebody who needs you today!

He says in this passage the spirit is willing but the flesh is weak. Our flesh never wants to do the things of God, but you as an ambassador of Christ, make a decision today to shake off that flesh and be led by the Spirit of God. Today shake your prayer life to another level! Stop reading this right now and go to praying for at least a good 10 minutes about those closest to you that their soul is vexed! Reach out to them, tell them you prayed for them, let them know God laid them on your heart. You never know what tomorrow brings for them or even the next few hours. Pray! Pray! Pray!

What did the words of Jesus speak to you today?

_____

_____

_____

_____

_____

How can you apply them to your life?

_____

_____

_____

_____

_____

Matthew 27
11 Now Jesus stood before the governor. And the governor asked Him, saying, "Are You the King of the Jews?" Jesus said to him, "It is as you say." 46 And about the ninth hour Jesus cried out with a loud voice, saying, "Eli, Eli, lama sabachthani?" that is, "My God, My God, why have You forsaken Me?" 63 saying, "Sir, we remember, while He was still alive, how that deceiver said, 'After three days I will rise.'

Matthew 28
9 And as they went to tell His disciples, behold, Jesus met them, saying, "Rejoice!" So they came and held Him by the feet and worshiped Him. 10 Then Jesus said to them, "Do not be afraid. Go and tell My brethren to go to Galilee, and there they will see Me." 18 And Jesus came and spoke to them, saying, "All authority has been given to Me in heaven and on earth. 19 Go therefore and make disciples of all the nations, baptizing them in the name of the Father and of the Son and of the Holy Spirit, 20 teaching them to observe all things that I have commanded you; and lo, I am with you always, even to the end of the age." Amen.

The Gospel of Mark
Mark 1
At the baptism of Jesus, in the River Jordan after the Holy Ghost descended

The Father spoke
11 Thou art my beloved Son, in whom I am well pleased.
In Galilee, to the people
15 The time is fulfilled, and the kingdom of God is at hand: repent ye, and believe the gospel.
By the Sea of Galilee, to Simon and Andrew
17 Come ye after me, and I will make you to become fishers of men. 18 And straightway they forsook their nets, and followed him.

In the synagogue at Capernaum, to an unclean spirit
25 Hold thy peace, and come out of him.

In a solitary place, to his disciples
38 Let us go into the next towns, that I may preach there also: for therefore came I forth.

In a Galilean synagogue, to a leper
41 I will; be thou clean. 44 See thou say nothing to any man: but go thy way, shew thyself to the priest, and offer for thy cleansing those things which Moses commanded, for a testimony unto them.

Mark 2
In a house at Capernaum, to one sick of palsy
5 Son, thy sins be forgiven thee.

In a house at Capernaum, to the scribes
8 Why reason ye these things in your hearts? 9 Whether is it easier to say to the sick of the palsy, Thy sins be forgiven thee; or to say, Arise, and take up thy bed, and walk? 10 But that ye may know that the Son of man hath power on earth to forgive sins, To the sick of the palsy 11 I say unto thee, Arise, and take up thy bed, and go thy way into thine house.

At the receipt of custom, to Levi
14 Follow me.

In Levi's house, to the scribes and Pharisees

17 They that are whole have no need of the physician, but they that are sick: I came not to call the righteous, but sinners to repentance. 18 And the disciples of John and of the Pharisees used to fast: and they come and say unto him, Why do the disciples of John and of the Pharisees fast, but thy disciples fast not? 19 Can the children of the bridechamber fast, while the bridegroom is with them? As long as they have the bridegroom with them, they cannot fast. 20 But the days will come, when the bridegroom shall be taken away from them, and then shall they fast in those days. 21 No man also seweth a piece of new cloth on an old garment: else the new piece that filled it up taketh away from the old, and the rent is made worse. 22 And no man putteth new wine into old bottles: else the new wine doth burst the bottles, and the wine is spilled, and the bottles will be marred: but new wine must be put into new bottles.

In the cornfield, on the Sabbath, to the Pharisees

25 Have ye never read what David did, when he had need, and was an hungered, he, and they that were with him? 26 How he went into the house of God in the days of Abiathar the high priest, and did eat the shewbread, which is not lawful to eat but for the priests, and gave also to them which were with him? 27 The Sabbath was made for man, and not man for the Sabbath: 28 therefore the Son of man is Lord also of the Sabbath.

Mark 3
In the synagogue, to a man with a withered hand

3 Stand forth.

In the synagogue, to the Pharisees

4 Is it lawful to do good on the Sabbath days, or to do evil? To save life, or to kill?

To the man with a withered hand

5 Stretch forth thine hand. And he stretched it out: and his hand was restored whole as the other.

To the scribes

23 And he called them unto him, and said unto them in parables, How can Satan cast out Satan? 24 And if a kingdom be divided against itself, that kingdom cannot stand. 25 And if a house be divided against itself, that house cannot stand. 26 And if Satan rise up against himself, and be divided, he cannot stand, but hath an end. 27 No man can enter into a strong man's house, and spoil his goods, except he will first bind the strong man; and then he will spoil his house. 28 Verily I say unto you, All sins shall be forgiven unto the sons of men, and blasphemies wherewith soever they shall blaspheme: 29 but he that shall blaspheme against the Holy Ghost hath never forgiveness, but is in danger of eternal damnation:

DEVOTION

Don't Lose Focus!

Matthew, Mark, Luke and John are all called the Gospels. They are four depictions of the life of Jesus written by four different people. Remember you're reading the words in red. Continue to get your Bible out and follow along!

Wow! Wow! Wow! Mark immediately goes into telling about how Jesus is the healer and a deliverer. Immediately he's casting demons out, cleansing lepers, healing paralysis, telling hands to stretch out, putting religious folk in their place and telling them He's the Lord of the Sabbath! They were focused on the outward motion and He was focused on miracles!

Today we want to talk to you about focus! Sometimes it's hard for us after we've been looking at something for a long time to really see what's in front of us. Many times we will stare out the window of our car watching the road and not even realizing that on our windshield we've got tons of marks or dirt. Your eyes then will make an adjustment and you will see what's right in front of you, turn on your windshield wipers and shoot out some fluid to clean the glass!

Jesus is telling us to stay focused…that He is a miracle worker and that when you follow Him you can expect the same! Blinded eyes will open, withered arms will stretch out, sick people will get healed and whatever's dirty will get clean! So don't look like the religious folk who are trying to put the new wine in the old wine skins. Throw those things away! Throw those traditions away! Jesus has provided a new wine for us!!

What did the words of Jesus speak to you today?

_____

_____

_____

_____

_____

How can you apply them to your life?

_____

_____

_____

_____

_____

To the multitude

33 Who is my mother, or my brethren? 34 And he looked round about on them which sat about him, Behold my mother and my brethren! 35 For whosoever shall do the will of God, the same is my brother, and my sister, and mother.

Mark 4

In a ship, by the sea side, to the multitude

3 Hearken; behold, there went out a sower to sow: 4 and it came to pass, as he sowed, some fell by the way side, and the fowls of the air came and devoured it up. 5 And some fell on stony ground, where it had not much earth; and immediately it sprang up, because it had no depth of earth: 6 but when the sun was up, it was scorched; and because it had no root, it withered away. 7 And some fell among thorns, and the thorns grew up, and choked it, and it yielded no fruit. 8 And other fell on good ground, and did yield fruit that sprang up and increased; and brought forth, some thirty, and some sixty, and some an hundred. 9He that hath ears to hear, let him hear.

To the disciples, concerning the parable

11Unto you it is given to know the mystery of the kingdom of God: but unto them that are without, all these things are done in parables: 12 that seeing they may see, and not perceive; and hearing they may hear, and not understand; lest at any time they should be converted, and their sins should be forgiven them 13 Know ye not this parable? And how then will ye know all parables? 14 The sower soweth the word. 15 And these are they by the way side, where the word is sown; but when they have heard, Satan cometh immediately, and taketh away the word that was sown in their hearts. 16 And these are they likewise which are sown on stony ground; who, when they have heard the word, immediately receive it with gladness; 17 and have no root in themselves, and so endure but for a time: afterward, when affliction or persecution ariseth for the word's sake, immediately they are offended.18 And these are they which are sown among thorns; such as hear the word, 19 and the cares of this world, and the deceitfulness of riches, and the lusts of other things entering in, choke the word, and it becometh unfruitful. 20 And these are they which are sown on good ground; such as hear the word, and receive it, and bring forth fruit, some thirtyfold, some sixty, and some an hundred. 21 Is a candle brought to be put under a bushel, or under a bed? And not to be set on a candlestick? 22 For there is nothing hid, which shall not be manifested; neither was any thing kept secret, but that it should come abroad. 23 If any man have ears to hear, let him hear.24 Take heed what ye hear: with what measure ye mete, it shall be measured to you: and unto you that hear shall more be given. 25 For he that hath, to him shall be given: and he that hath not, from him shall be taken even that which he hath. 26 So is the kingdom of God, as if a man should cast seed into the ground; 27 and should sleep, and rise night and day, and the seed should spring and grow up, he knoweth not how. 28 For the earth bringeth forth fruit of herself; first the blade, then the ear, after that the full corn in the ear. 29 But when the fruit is brought forth, immediately he putteth in the sickle, because the harvest is come.

30 Whereunto shall we liken the kingdom of God? Or with what comparison shall we compare it? 31 It is like a grain of mustard seed, which, when it is sown in the earth, is less than all the seeds that be in the earth: 32 but when it is sown, it groweth up, and becometh greater than all herbs, and shooteth out great branches; so that the fowls of the air may lodge under the shadow of it. 35 Let us pass over unto the other side.

On a ship, to the wind and sea

39 Peace, be still. And the wind ceased, and there was a great calm.

On the same ship, to the disciples

40 Why are ye so fearful? How is it that ye have no faith?

Mark 5
In the country of the Gadarenes, to the unclean spirit
8 Come out of the man, thou unclean spirit. 9 What is thy name? And he answered, saying, My name is Legion: for we are many.

To the man from the country of the Gadarenes who had the unclean spirit cast out
19 Go home to thy friends, and tell them how great things the Lord hath done for thee, and hath had compassion on thee.

On the way to Jairus' house, to the crowd
30 Who touched my clothes?

To the woman who touched him
34 Daughter, thy faith hath made thee whole; go in peace, and be whole of thy plague.

To Jairus
36 Be not afraid, only believe.

At the house of Jairus, to them that wept
39 Why make ye this ado, and weep? The damsel is not dead, but sleepeth.

To the damsel
41 Talitha cumi; (Damsel, I say unto thee, arise)

DEVOTION

No Faith, Little Faith, GREAAAATTTT FAITH - Your Faith?

Again, remember the Gospels say the same things sometimes, such as in Mark 5 with the parable of the seed.

Direct your attention to Mark 4:24. Unto you that hear, more will be given! What this means here is understanding! When we properly understand how the kingdom works, the result is increase! We are to have a measure of faith operating inside of us. Often, we say in church to measure our faith level. People with no faith sit back on their chair trying to fight sleep as they listen to the word. People with little faith are sitting up pondering and wondering how this faith thing works for them. But you can always spot the great faith!!! These are the ones that are on the edge of their chair, knees popping up and down, waiting for a moment to where they can stand and agree that that belongs to them. These are the ones that show up early and stay late. These are the ones that grab a hold of every word in the Bible and believe it belongs to them! You don't have to talk them into believing the word, they are walking in it! FAITH IS AN INWARD CONVICTION THAT DEMANDS AN OUTWARD ACT! BELIEVE- RECEIVE!

He asked the disciples in verse 40, "Why is it that you have no faith?", then turns around and tells the woman, "Your faith has made you whole". We see that there are levels of faith that people function in, then we see the key in Mark 5:36...don't fear - ONLY BELIEVE!

Get ready! Increase your faith level! Go to church on fire with a passion to believe IT CAN HAPPEN! Faith infusion!! You won't need anyone to tell you God can do it if you already know!

Just like you sit down on a chair without thinking, do the same with your faith! Don't think or reason, just believe!!! That word believe is *pistis* in the Greek - FULLY PERSUADED!

Say this out loud! I AM FULLY PERSUADED THAT GOD IS ENOUGH FOR ME! GOD, I INCREASE MY FAITH! NO LONGER WILL I SIT ON THE SIDELINES AND DO NOTHING BUT WATCH! I WILL RECEIVE AND MOVE IN THE KINGDOM!!

What did the words of Jesus speak to you today?

_____
_____
_____
_____
_____

How can you apply them to your life?

_____
_____
_____
_____
_____

Chapter 6
In the synagogue of his own country, to the people
4 A prophet is not without honour, but in his own country, and among his own kin, and in his own house.

To his disciples
10 In what place soever ye enter into an house, there abide till ye depart from that place. 11 And whosoever shall not receive you, nor hear you, when ye depart thence, shake off the dust under your feet for a testimony against them. Verily I say unto you, It shall be more tolerable for Sodom and Gomorrha in the day of judgment, than for that city.

To the apostles
31 Come ye yourselves apart into a desert place, and rest a while:

In a desert place, to his disciples
37 Give ye them to eat.
38 How many loaves have ye? Go and see.

On the sea, to his disciples
50 Be of good cheer: it is I; be not afraid.

Mark 7
In the land of Gennesaret, to the Pharisees and scribes
6 Well hath Esaias prophesied of you hypocrites, as it is written, this people honoureth me with their lips, but their heart is far from me. 7 Howbeit in vain do they worship me, teaching for doctrines the commandments of men. 8 For laying aside the commandment of God, ye hold the tradition of men, as the washing of pots and cups: and many other such like things ye do. 9 Full well ye reject the commandment of God, that ye may keep your own tradition. 10 For Moses said, Honour thy father and thy mother; and, Whoso curseth father or mother, let him die the death: 11 but ye say, If a man shall say to his father or mother, It is Corban, that is to say, a gift, by whatsoever thou mightest be profited by me; he shall be free.
12 And ye suffer him no more to do ought for his father or his mother; 13 making the word of God of none effect through your tradition, which ye have delivered: and many such like things do ye.

In the same region, to the people
14 Hearken unto me every one of you, and understand:
15 there is nothing from without a man that entering into him can defile him: but the things which come out of him, those are they that defile the man. 16 If any man have ears to hear, let him hear.

In a house, to his disciples
18 Are ye so without understanding also? Do ye not perceive, that whatsoever thing from without entereth into the man, it cannot defile him; 19 because it entereth not into his heart, but into the belly, and goeth out into the draught, purging all meats? 20 That which cometh out of the man, that defileth the man. 21 For from within, out of the heart of men, proceed evil thoughts, adulteries, fornications, murders, 22 thefts, covetousness, wickedness, deceit, lasciviousness, an evil eye, blasphemy, pride, foolishness: 23 all these evil things come from within, and defile the man.

In a house on the borders of Tyre and Sidon, to a Syrophenician woman
27 Let the children first be filled: for it is not meet to take the children's bread, and to cast it unto the dogs.

29 For this saying go thy way; the devil is gone out of thy daughter.

At the Sea of Galilee, on the coast of Decapolis, to a deaf man
34 Ephphatha, (Be opened)

DEVOTION

Hard WIRED!

Pharisees and scribes were religious people in the day of Jesus. Mark 7 - "These people honor me with their lips but their heart is far from me".

Jesus goes on to talk about how they honor their father and mother. He pretty much says you guys look for "loopholes" in the covenant. You honor with your lips but your heart has no action. He tells them that honoring your parents is more than just saying nice things about them. When you love, you don't just love with lips, you love with your heart and your deeds. Let me to stop here and talk to you about people who talk about their parents! If they can talk bad about their parents, that's a strong indication they won't have trouble talking about you! But the truth of the matter here is Jesus tells them that Elijah spoke about you all! Your reputation already precedes you. You're nothing but lip service. The engine is running but the transmission is not in gear. LOVE AND HONOR COMES WITH ACTION! People who talk only, can fool others but can't fool God! Out of the heart flows the issues of life. Your heart determines what happens through you!

Let your heart be full of Jesus! Let your heart get wired! When you are full of Jesus things will become automatic for you. Back in the day you could start a car by rubbing two wires together underneath the dash. You could bypass having a key. A matter of fact, no key was necessary if the two wires were hardwired together. All you had to do was tie them up and the car would start! This is what needs to happen to your heart concerning the covenant principles of God. You don't have to work or labor to love or have the right heart when you're in Jesus. "You will know them by their fruit" is what Jesus says. A tree doesn't work hard to produce fruit, it just stays in the soil and whatever's in the vine comes out through the branches. HARDWIRED!

What did the words of Jesus speak to you today?

_____
_____
_____
_____
_____

How can you apply them to your life?

_____
_____
_____
_____
_____

To his disciples
Mark 8
2 I have compassion on the multitude, because they have now been with me three days, and have nothing to eat: 3 and if I send them away fasting to their own houses, they will faint by the way: for divers of them came from far.
5 How many loaves have ye?

In Dalmanutha, to the Pharisees
12 Why doth this generation seek after a sign? Verily I say unto you, There shall no sign be given unto this generation.

In a ship, to his disciples
15 Take heed, beware of the leaven of the Pharisees, and of the leaven of Herod. 17 Why reason ye, because ye have no bread? Perceive ye not yet, neither understand? Have ye your heart yet hardened? 18 Having eyes, see ye not? And having ears, hear ye not? And do ye not remember? 19 When I brake the five loaves among five thousand, how many baskets full of fragments took ye up?

They say unto him, Twelve.
20 And when the seven among four thousand, how many baskets full of fragments took ye up? And they said, Seven. 21 How is it that ye do not understand?

In Bethsaida, to a man healed of blindness
26 Neither go into the town, nor tell it to any in the town.

In Caesarea Philippi, to his disciples
27 Whom do men say that I am?
29 But whom say ye that I am?

In Caesarea Philippi, to Peter
33 Get thee behind me, Satan: for thou savourest not the things that be of God, but the things that be of men.

In Caesarea Philippi, to the people and his disciples
34 Whosoever will come after me, let him deny himself, and take up his cross, and follow me. 35 For whosoever will save his life shall lose it; but whosoever shall lose his life for my sake and the gospel's, the same shall save it. 36 For what shall it profit a man, if he shall gain the whole world, and lose his own soul? 37 Or what shall a man give in exchange for his soul? 38 Whosoever therefore shall be ashamed of me and of my words in this adulterous and sinful generation; of him also shall the Son of man be ashamed, when he cometh in the glory of his Father with the holy angels.

Mark 9
1 Verily I say unto you, That there be some of them that stand here, which shall not taste of death, till they have seen the kingdom of God come with power.

At the transfiguration of Jesus in a high mountain
The Father spoke
7 This is my beloved Son: hear him.

After his transfiguration, to Peter, James and John
12 Elias verily cometh first, and restoreth all things; and how it is written of the Son of man, that he must suffer many things, and be set at nought. 13 But I say unto you, That Elias is indeed come, and they have done unto him whatsoever they listed, as it is written of him.

To the scribes questioning with the multitude
16 What question ye with them?

To his disciples concerning the father of a possessed child
19 O faithless generation, how long shall I be with you? How long shall I suffer you? Bring him unto me.

To the father of a possessed child
21 How long is it ago since this came unto him? 23If thou canst believe, all things are possible to him that believeth.

To the foul spirit
25 Thou dumb and deaf spirit, I charge thee, come out of him, and enter no more into him.

In a house, to his disciples
29 This kind can come forth by nothing, but by prayer and fasting.

DEVOTION

I'm Sorry. Can You Repeat That?

Have you ever had somebody around you that could hear well but wouldn't listen well!?? 20/20 hearing but they wouldn't listen! Have you ever had a conversation with somebody that as you were looking at them, they were preoccupied with something else and you knew the more you talked to them, you were fooling yourself that they were actually listening? "What did you say?" "Can you repeat that?" "I'm sorry, can you say that again?" The whole time they have the conversation with you they make noises like, "mhmmm, yessss, right...." nod their head but are distracted, haven't heard a word!!

This is how Jesus felt because His disciples had seen the miracles but yet they were not seeing the kingdom. He says on a ship in Mark 8:18, "You have eyes and you can't see, you have ears and you can't hear. I've shown you what I can do but yet you keep questioning me. Why are you so distracted? What are you thinking? The kingdom is right now and the miracles are happening yet you were still trying to reason if it's possible"!

Now before we get all high-minded about the disciples, how many times have we reasoned in ourselves that the miracle we needed was not possible? I truly believe that the enemy of faith is not always fear. Sometimes the enemy of faith is reason. You can't budget God. You can't put a lid on God. The Bible says with God, ALL THINGS ARE POSSIBLE! Do you know what the Greek is for the word "ALL"? (Brace yourself...huge revelation here....). It's ALL!! Everything! It encompasses your situation. HE'S ABLE! That's never the issue. The issue is, are we willing to WALK IN HIS KINGDOM! Remember, if you understand, MORE (increase) will be given!

"I'm sorry can you repeat that?" The good thing about Jesus is that He will...until we get it. Lord increase our faith!

What did the words of Jesus speak to you today?

_____

_____

_____

_____

_____

How can you apply them to your life?

_____

_____

_____

_____

_____

In Galilee, to his disciples
31 The Son of man is delivered into the hands of men, and they shall kill him; and after that he is killed, he shall rise the third day.

In a house at Capernaum, to his disciples
33 What was it that ye disputed among yourselves by the way? 35 If any man desire to be first, the same shall be last of all, and servant of all. 37 Whosoever shall receive one of such children in my name, receiveth me: and whosoever shall receive me, receiveth not me, but him that sent me.

To John the Apostle
39 Forbid him not: for there is no man which shall do a miracle in my name, that can lightly speak evil of me. 40 For he that is not against us is on our part. 41 For whosoever shall give you a cup of water to drink in my name, because ye belong to Christ, verily I say unto you, he shall not lose his reward. 42 And whosoever shall offend one of these little ones that believe in me, it is better for him that a millstone were hanged about his neck, and he were cast into the sea. 43 And if thy hand offend thee, cut it off: it is better for thee to enter into life maimed, than having two hands to go into hell, into the fire that never shall be quenched: 44 where their worm dieth not, and the fire is not quenched. 45 And if thy foot offend thee, cut it off: it is better for thee to enter halt into life, than having two feet to be cast into hell, into the fire that never shall be quenched: 46 where their worm dieth not, and the fire is not quenched. 47 And if thine eye offend thee, pluck it out: it is better for thee to enter into the kingdom of God with one eye, than having two eyes to be cast into hell fire: 48 where their worm dieth not, and the fire is not quenched. 49 For every one shall be salted with fire, and every sacrifice shall be salted with salt.50 Salt is good: but if the salt have lost his saltness, wherewith will ye season it? Have salt in yourselves, and have peace one with another.

Mark 10
In the coasts of Judea by the farther side of Jordan, to the Pharisees
3 What did Moses command you? 5 For the hardness of your heart he wrote you this precept. 6 But from the beginning of the creation God made them male and female. 7 For this cause shall a man leave his father and mother, and cleave to his wife; 8 and they twain shall be one flesh: so then they are no more twain, but one flesh.9 What therefore God hath joined together, let not man put asunder.
In the house, to his disciples 11 Whosoever shall put away his wife, and marry another, committeth adultery against her. 12 And if a woman shall put away her husband, and be married to another, she committeth adultery. 14 Suffer the little children to come unto me, and forbid them not: for of such is the kingdom of God. 15 Verily I say unto you, Whosoever shall not receive the kingdom of God as a little child, he shall not enter therein.

To a rich man
18 Why callest thou me good? There is none good but one, that is, God. 19 Thou knowest the commandments, Do not commit adultery, Do not kill, Do not steal, Do not bear false witness, Defraud not,

Honour thy father and mother.
21 One thing thou lackest: go thy way, sell whatsoever thou hast, and give to the poor, and thou shalt have treasure in heaven: and come, take up the cross, and follow me.
To his disciples 23 How hardly shall they that have riches enter into the kingdom of God! 24 Children, how hard is it for them that trust in riches to enter into the kingdom of God! 25 It is easier for a camel to go through the eye of a needle, than for a rich man to enter into the kingdom of God. 27 With men it is impossible, but not with God: for with God all things are possible. 29

Verily I say unto you, There is no man that hath left house, or brethren, or sisters, or father, or mother, or wife, or children, or lands, for my sake, and the gospel's, 30 but he shall receive an hundredfold now in this time, houses, and brethren, and sisters, and mothers, and children, and lands, with persecutions; and in the world to come eternal life. 31 But many that are first shall be last; and the last first.

DEVOTION

Cut It Off!!

Satan has a system:
1. Temptation
2. Drawn away
3. Personal lust
4. Enticement
5. LUST CONCEIVED
6. BIRTH TO SIN
7. CONSEQUENCES

Satan has a method. The Bible says to stand against the wiles of the devil. Wiles are "schemes, methods, SYSTEMS.

Jesus is speaking metaphorically here about cutting your hand off, poking your eyes out and cutting your feet off. We know that it is metaphoric because He says "it would be better to enter the kingdom of heaven maimed…" No one is going to be walking around heaven maimed or without an arm or leg! Jesus is making a principle here:

Above, I put in ALL CAPS where sin actually conceives. Many people think because they were tempted that they have already sinned but if that was the case, Jesus sinned when He was in the wilderness and tempted. Sin happens when the spiritual gives birth in the natural..."CONCEIVED!" Everything before that is temptation. The key here is to take away whatever is creating the appetite for your CONTINUAL sin to keep happening! Jesus is simply saying that it may be something very special or precious to you, however it would be better for you to lose that here on earth than to go to hell eternally.

Today, take inventory of what are the triggers that continually draw you into sin. That thing may be a person, it may be a bottle, it may be a conversation that you continually have. Get aggressive! CUT IT OFF!! Drop it! Open the window of your house and tell that thing to leave! Command it to go! If it's money, give it away! If it's a man or a woman, cut them off! Whatever it is that keeps you thirsty for sin, SPIRITUALY KILL IT!! Let it wither and don't try and attach it back again!!

What did the words of Jesus speak to you today?

_____
_____
_____
_____
_____

How can you apply them to your life?

_____

_____

_____

_____

_____

On the way to Jerusalem, to his disciples
33 Behold, we go up to Jerusalem; and the Son of man shall be delivered unto the chief priests, and unto the scribes; and they shall condemn him to death, and shall deliver him to the Gentiles: 34 and they shall mock him, and shall scourge him, and shall spit upon him, and shall kill him: and the third day he shall rise again.

To James and John
36 What would ye that I should do for you?
38 Ye know not what ye ask: can ye drink of the cup that I drink of? And be baptized with the baptism that I am baptized with? 39 Ye shall indeed drink of the cup that I drink of; and with the baptism that I am baptized withal shall ye be baptized: 40 but to sit on my right hand and on my left hand is not mine to give; but it shall be given to them for whom it is prepared.

To the other ten disciples
42 Ye know that they which are accounted to rule over the gentiles exercise lordship over them; and their great ones exercise authority upon them. 43 But so shall it not be among you: but whosoever will be great among you, shall be your minister: 44 and whosoever of you will be the chiefest, shall be servant of all. 45 For even the Son of man came not to be ministered unto, but to minister, and to give his life a ransom for many.

In Jericho, to blind Bartimaeus
51 What wilt thou that I should do unto thee? 52 Go thy way; thy faith hath made thee whole.

Mark 11
At the Mount of Olives, to two of his disciples
2 Go your way into the village over against you: and as soon as ye be entered into it, ye shall find a colt tied, whereon never man sat; loose him, and bring him. 3 And if any man say unto you, Why do ye this? Say ye that the Lord hath need of him; and straightway he will send him hither.

On his way to Jerusalem, to a fig tree
14 No man eat fruit of thee hereafter forever.

In Jerusalem's temple, to them that bought and sold in the temple
17 Is it not written, My house shall be called of all nations the house of prayer? But ye have made it a den of thieves.

By the cursed fig tree, to his disciples
22 Have faith in God. 23 For verily I say unto you, That whosoever shall say unto this mountain, Be thou removed, and be thou cast into the sea; and shall not doubt in his heart, but shall believe that those things which he saith shall come to pass; he shall have whatsoever he saith. 24 Therefore I say unto you, What things soever ye desire, when ye pray, believe that ye receive them, and ye shall have them. 25 And when ye stand praying, forgive, if ye have ought against any: that your Father also which is in heaven may forgive you your trespasses. 26 But if ye do not forgive, neither will your Father which is in heaven forgive your trespasses.

In Jerusalem's temple, to the chief priests and scribes
29 I will also ask of you one question, and answer me, and I will tell you by what authority I do these things. 30 The baptism of John, was it from heaven, or of men? answer me.
33 Neither do I tell you by what authority I do these things.

Mark 12

1 And he began to speak unto them by parables. A certain man planted a vineyard, and set an hedge about it, and digged a place for the winefat, and built a tower, and let it out to husbandmen, and went into a far country. 2 And at the season he sent to the husbandmen a servant, that he might receive from the husbandmen of the fruit of the vineyard. 3 And they caught him, and beat him, and sent him away empty. 4 And again he sent unto them another servant; and at him they cast stones, and wounded him in the head, and sent him away shamefully handled. 5 And again he sent another; and him they killed, and many others; beating some, and killing some. 6 Having yet therefore one son, his well beloved, he sent him also last unto them, saying, They will reverence my son. 7 But those husbandmen said among themselves, This is the heir; come, let us kill him, and the inheritance shall be ours. 8 And they took him, and killed him, and cast him out of the vineyard. 9 What shall therefore the lord of the vineyard do? He will come and destroy the husbandmen, and will give the vineyard unto others. 10 And have ye not read this scripture; The stone which the builders rejected is become the head of the corner: 11 this was the Lord's doing, and it is marvelous in our eyes?

DEVOTION

Fig Tree Religion

Mark 11:14 is one of the greatest revelations God ever gave me concerning my relationship with Him.

What was the first thing that happened after the serpent had deceived Adam and Eve? The first thing they did was realize they were naked and they went and covered themselves with leaves. Genesis 3:7 says they were not just any leaves, they were fig leaves. God spoke to me and told me that when people break relationship and go after religion this is what happens. When we cover ourselves with "fig leaves" it is simply because we realize what we have done. So what do we do? When we sin the first thing we try to do is try and cover ourselves. That's the first thing sin made them realize...you're uncovered! So we go and try to make ourselves feel better by covering our issues instead of cleansing them.

Jesus saw the fig tree and was looking for fruit. Others may have been impressed by the leaves but Jesus never is impressed by what we put on the outward...He is always looking for fruit. He didn't curse the fig tree because he was upset and was hungry, He cursed the fig tree because it was not bearing fruit. Wow! God is always looking for our fruit not our leaves. He even goes to say in the RED words, "You shall know they are my disciples because of their fruit...their love"! Today, choose to go after the fruit of the Spirit just as much as you go after the gifts! Make your fruit grow so big that it overshadows anything else in your life. Love, joy, peace, patience, kindness, goodness, faithfulness, gentleness and self-control!

What did the words of Jesus speak to you today?

_____

_____

_____

_____

_____

How can you apply them to your life?

_____

_____

_____

_____

_____

To the Pharisees and the Herodians
15 Why tempt ye me? Bring me a penny, that I may see it.
16 Whose is this image and superscription? 17 Render to Caesar the things that are Caesar's, and to God the things that are God's.

To the Sadducees
24 Do ye not therefore err, because ye know not the scriptures, neither the power of God? 25 For when they shall rise from the dead, they neither marry, nor are given in marriage; but are as the angels which are in heaven. 26 And as touching the dead, that they rise: have ye not read in the book of Moses, how in the bush God spake unto him, saying, I am the God of Abraham, and the God of Isaac, and the God of Jacob? 27 He is not the God of the dead, but the God of the living: ye therefore do greatly err.

To one of the scribes
29 The first of all the commandments is, Hear, O Israel; The Lord our God is one Lord: 30 and thou shalt love the Lord thy God with all thy heart, and with all thy soul, and with all thy mind, and with all thy strength: this is the first commandment. 31 And the second is like, namely this, Thou shalt love thy neighbour as thyself. There is none other commandment greater than these. 34 Thou art not far from the kingdom of God.

In the temple, to the people
35 How say the scribes that Christ is the Son of David? 36 For David himself said by the Holy Ghost, The Lord said to my Lord, Sit thou on my right hand, till I make thine enemies thy footstool. 37 David therefore himself calleth him Lord; and whence is he then his son? 38 Beware of the scribes, which love to go in long clothing, and love salutations in the marketplaces, 39 and the chief seats in the synagogues, and the uppermost rooms at feasts: 40 which devour widows' houses, and for a pretence make long prayers: these shall receive greater damnation.

Near the treasury in the temple, to his disciples
43 Verily I say unto you, That this poor widow hath cast more in, than all they which have cast into the treasury: 44 for all they did cast in of their abundance; but she of her want did cast in all that she had, even all her living.

Mark 13
By Jerusalem's temple, to one of his disciples
2 Seest thou these great buildings? There shall not be left one stone upon another, that shall not be thrown down.

On the Mount of Olives, to Peter, James, John and Andrew
5 Take heed lest any man deceive you: 6 for many shall come in my name, saying, I am Christ; and shall deceive many. 7 And when ye shall hear of wars and rumors of wars, be ye not troubled: for such things must needs be; but the end shall not be yet. 8 For nation shall rise against nation, and kingdom against kingdom: and there shall be earthquakes in divers places, and there shall be famines and troubles: these are the beginnings of sorrows. 9 But take heed to yourselves: for they shall deliver you up to councils; and in the synagogues ye shall be beaten: and ye shall be brought before rulers and kings for my sake, for a testimony against them. 10 And the gospel must first be published among all nations. 11 But when they shall lead you, and deliver you up, take no thought beforehand what ye shall speak, neither do ye premeditate: but whatsoever shall be given you in that hour that speak ye: for it is not ye that speak, but the Holy Ghost. 12 Now the brother shall

betray the brother to death, and the father the son; and children shall rise up against their parents, and shall cause them to be put to death. 13 And ye shall be hated of all men for my name's sake: but he that shall endure unto the end, the same shall be saved. 14 But when ye shall see the abomination of desolation, spoken of by Daniel the prophet, standing where it ought not, (let him that readeth understand,) then let them that be in Judaea flee to the mountains: 15 and let him that is on the housetop not go down into the house, neither enter therein, to take anything out of his house: 16 and let him that is in the field not turn back again for to take up his garment. 17 But woe to them that are with child, and to them that give suck in those days! 18 And pray ye that your flight be not in the winter. 19 For in those days shall be affliction, such as was not from the beginning of the creation which God created unto this time, neither shall be. 20 And except that the Lord had shortened those days, no flesh should be saved: but for the elect's sake, whom he hath chosen, he hath shortened the days. 21 And then if any man shall say to you, Lo, here is Christ; or, lo, he is there; believe him not: 22 for false Christs and false prophets shall rise, and shall shew signs and wonders, to seduce, if it were possible, even the elect.
23 But take ye heed: behold, I have foretold you all things.
24 But in those days, after that tribulation, the sun shall be darkened, and the moon shall not give her light, 25 and the stars of heaven shall fall, and the powers that are in heaven shall be shaken. 26 And then shall they see the Son of man coming in the clouds with great power and glory. 27 And then shall he send his angels, and shall gather together his elect from the four winds, from the uttermost part of the earth to the uttermost part of heaven. 28 Now learn a parable of the fig tree; When her branch is yet tender, and putteth forth leaves, ye know that summer is near: 29 so ye in like manner, when ye shall see these things come to pass, know that it is nigh, even at the doors. 30 Verily I say unto you, that this generation shall not pass, till all these things be done. 31 Heaven and earth shall pass away: but my words shall not pass away. 32 But of that day and that hour knoweth no man, no, not the angels which are in heaven, neither the Son, but the Father. 33 Take ye heed, watch and pray: for ye know not when the time is. 34 For the Son of man is as a man taking a far journey, who left his house, and gave authority to his servants, and to every man his work, and commanded the porter to watch. 35 Watch ye therefore: for ye know not when the master of the house cometh, at even, or at midnight, or at the cockcrowing, or in the morning: 36 lest coming suddenly he find you sleeping. 37 And what I say unto you I say unto all, Watch.

DEVOTION

Loves Me...Loves Me Not...

Remember when we were kids and we would pick a daisy in the field? We would pull each petal in order to find out if a person loved us or not. We would pull one petal and we'd say "He loves me or she loves me…", then we would pull the next petal and we would say "He loves me not or she loves me not". We'd get to the last petal and when we pulled it whatever was in sequence was the answer we were looking for. We were hoping for the best and hoping that when we pulled that last petal, this game of chance was our decision!

Not so in the kingdom of God. Jesus tells us in day 22 reading the words in Mark 12:29, that we are to love God, love our neighbor and then He says at the end of it AS OURSELF! In other words, we're going to have a hard time loving others if we can't accept ourselves. Every day we tend to pull a petal when we wake up in the morning concerning ourselves. If we love ourselves everybody else will be loved! We will treat everybody wonderful! But if we pull an "I love me not" petal, we will grumble and complain and blame and hate everything about our day.

A healthy love for our neighbor starts with a healthy love for ourselves. It's hard to love everybody else when you hate yourself! So many people in this world cut themselves, look in the mirror and call themselves fat or stupid or just simply have been told so much that they're worth nothing that they actually have believed it and say it about themselves. Today, LOVE YOUSELF! Let's explain that.

Shame and guilt are the evil twins of grace and mercy! Today throw your shame and throw your guilt at the feet of Jesus and ask Jesus to help you love yourself again beyond all your mistakes and your pain. Watch how much you will begin to love others! Sometimes it's easy to love God yet it's very hard to love ourselves because we know more than anybody else what we have done. Let it go! Live abundantly!

What did the words of Jesus speak to you today?

_____
_____
_____
_____
_____

How can you apply them to your life?

_____
_____
_____
_____
_____

Mark 14
At Bethany, in Simon the leper's house, to his disciples
6 Let her alone; why trouble ye her? She hath wrought a good work on me. 7 For ye have the poor with you always, and whensoever ye will ye may do them good: but me ye have not always. 8 She hath done what she could: she is come aforehand to anoint my body to the burying. 9 Verily I say unto you, Wheresoever this gospel shall be preached throughout the whole world, this also that she hath done shall be spoken of for a memorial of her.

On the first day of Passover, to two of his disciples
13 Go ye into the city, and there shall meet you a man bearing a pitcher of water: follow him. 14 And wheresoever he shall go in, say ye to the goodman of the house, The Master saith, Where is the guest chamber, where I shall eat the passover with my disciples? 15 And he will shew you a large upper room furnished and prepared: there make ready for us.

At the Passover supper in the upper room, to his twelve
18 Verily I say unto you, One of you which eateth with me shall betray me. 20 It is one of the twelve, that dippeth with me in the dish. 21 The Son of man indeed goeth, as it is written of him: but woe to that man by whom the Son of man is betrayed! Good were it for that man if he had never been born. 22 And as they did eat, Jesus took bread, and blessed, and brake it, and gave to them take, eat: this is my body. 23 And he took the cup, and when he had given thanks, he gave it to them: and they all drank of it. 24 This is my blood of the New Testament, which is shed for many. 25 Verily I say unto you, I will drink no more of the fruit of the vine, until that day that I drink it new in the kingdom of God.

At the Mount of Olives, to his disciples
27 All ye shall be offended because of me this night: for it is written, I will smite the shepherd, and the sheep shall be scattered. 28 But after that I am risen, I will go before you into Galilee.

To Peter
30 Verily I say unto thee, That this day, even in this night, before the cock crow twice, thou shalt deny me thrice.

At Gethsemane, to his disciples
32 Sit ye here, while I shall pray.

At Gethsemane, to Peter, James and John
34 My soul is exceeding sorrowful unto death: tarry ye here, and watch.

Praying in the garden, to the Father
36 Abba, Father, all things are possible unto thee; take away this cup from me: nevertheless not what I will, but what thou wilt.

In Gethsemane, to Peter
37 Simon, sleepest thou? Couldest not thou watch one hour? 38 Watch ye and pray, lest ye enter into temptation. The spirit truly is ready, but the flesh is

In Gethsemane, to Peter, James and John
41 Sleep on now, and take your rest: it is enough, the hour is come; behold, the Son of man is betrayed into the hands of sinners. 42 Rise up, let us go; lo, he that betrayeth me is at hand.

To the multitude who were with Judas the betrayer
48 Are ye come out, as against a thief, with swords and with staves to take me? 49 I was daily with you in the temple teaching, and ye took me not: but the scriptures must be fulfilled.

In the palace of the high priest, to the high priest
62 I am: and ye shall see the Son of man sitting on the right hand of power, and coming in the clouds of heaven.

Mark 15
To Pilate, when asked, "Art thou the King of the Jews?"
2 Thou sayest it.

On the cross, to his Father
34 Eloi, Eloi, lama sabachthani? (My God, my God, why hast thou forsaken me?)

Mark 16
In Galilee, to his eleven disciples before he was received up into heaven, and seated at the right hand of God 15 Go ye into all the world, and preach the gospel to every creature. 16 He that believeth and is baptized shall be saved; but he that believeth not shall be damned. 17 And these signs shall follow them that believe; In my name shall they cast out devils; they shall speak with new tongues; 18 they shall take up serpents; and if they drink any deadly thing, it shall not hurt them; they shall lay hands on the sick, and they shall recover.

DEVOTION

Something is Following You!

Mark 16:17, "And these signs shall follow them that believe"!

Hallelujah! Did you just read that? It says that when we are a believer something is following us! The word follow in the Greek is hautos, which really means accompany! It is also where we get the word "auto".

Most people don't know what a stick shift is in the car because we're so used to our car shifting on its own. It's called an automatic transmission. However, back in the day you would have to push the clutch down and shift it yourself. But because you have an automatic transmission you don't have to do all that work!

When you pray for the sick or cast out demons it should be automatic! The Bible says the signs accompany the believer! And then He goes on to say "they will" recover. There is no doubt about this scripture that when we pray for things we should expect them to happen, in the name of Jesus! We shouldn't have to work real hard about it or shift it or labor with it. These things should be as automatic as your car while you're driving down the road...it shifts from 1st to 2nd without you even paying attention to it.

Try this! Try today! Go after it and pray for somebody who's sick. Believe the words of Jesus! Watch your faith in His words, and not your words, create automatic blessings and automatic healings! Something is accompanying you every day of your life. The Holy Spirit is inside of you ready and willing to work the works of God through you! When that happens be sure to give God all the praise!

What did the words of Jesus speak to you today?

_____

_____

_____

_____

_____

How can you apply them to your life?

_____

_____

_____

_____

_____

The Gospel According to Luke
Luke 2
In Jerusalem's temple, to his parents
49 How is it that ye sought me? Wist ye not that I must be about my Father's business?

Luke 3
At the baptism of Jesus, after the Holy Ghost descended The Father spoke 22 Thou art my
beloved Son; in thee I am well pleased.

Luke 4
In the wilderness, to Satan
*4 It is written, that man shall not live by bread alone, but by every word of God. 8 Get thee behind
me, Satan: for it is written, Thou shalt worship the Lord thy God, and him only shalt thou serve. 12
It is said, Thou shalt not tempt the Lord thy God.*

In Nazareth's synagogue, on the Sabbath, from the book of Esaias
*18 The Spirit of the Lord is upon me, because he hath anointed me to preach the gospel to the poor;
he hath sent me to heal the brokenhearted, to preach deliverance to the captives, and recovering of
sight to the blind, to set at liberty them that are bruised, 19 to preach the acceptable year of the
Lord.*

To all those in Nazareth's synagogue
21 This day is this scripture fulfilled in your ears.
*23 Ye will surely say unto me this proverb, Physician, heal thyself: whatsoever we have heard done
in Capernaum, do also here in thy country. 24 Verily I say unto you, No prophet is accepted in his
own country. 25 But I tell you of a truth, many widows were in Israel in the days of Elias, when the
heaven was shut up three years and six months, when great famine was throughout all the land; 26
but unto none of them was Elias sent, save unto Sarepta, a city of Sidon, unto a woman that was a
widow. 27 And many lepers were in Israel in the time of Eliseus the prophet; and none of them was
cleansed, saving Naaman the Syrian.*

In Capernaum, in the synagogue, to an unclean devil
35 Hold thy peace, and come out of him.

In a desert place, to the people
43 I must preach the kingdom of God to other cities also: for therefore am I sent.

Luke 5
At the lake of Gennesaret, to Simon
*4 Launch out into the deep, and let down your nets for a draught. 10 Fear not; from henceforth
thou shalt catch men.*

In a certain city, to a man with leprosy
*13 I will: be thou clean. And immediately the leprosy departed from him 14 And he charged him to
tell no man: but go, and shew thyself to the priest, and offer for thy cleansing, according as Moses
commanded, for a testimony unto them.*

To a man taken with a palsy
20 Man, thy sins are forgiven thee.

To the scribes and Pharisees
22 What reason ye in your hearts? 23 Whether is easier, to say, Thy sins be forgiven thee; or to say, Rise up and walk? 24 But that ye may know that the Son of man hath power upon earth to forgive sins,

To the sick of palsy
I say unto thee, Arise, and take up thy couch, and go into thine house.

At the receipt of custom, to Levi
27 Follow me.

In Levi's house, to the scribes and Pharisees
31 They that are whole need not a physician; but they that are sick. 32 I came not to call the righteous, but sinners to repentance. 34 Can ye make the children of the bridechamber fast, while the bridegroom is with them? 35 But the days will come, when the bridegroom shall be taken away from them, and then shall they fast in those days. 36 No man putteth a piece of a new garment upon an old; if otherwise, then both the new maketh a rent, and the piece that was taken out of the new agreeth not with the old. 37 And no man putteth new wine into old bottles; else the new wine will burst the bottles, and be spilled, and the bottles shall perish. 38 But new wine must be put into new bottles; and both are preserved. 39 No man also having drunk old wine straightway desireth new: for he saith, The old is better.

DEVOTION

The "Job Description" of Jesus

Already in the Gospel of Luke, remember there are four depictions of the life of Jesus so it's going to feel like you've already read this but keep re-reading, it gets so good!!

Luke 2:18, Jesus says what He came to do. Maybe I missed something but I don't see anywhere where He said condemn or hold grudges, leave people out or look down on those that are not good enough. Actually He says, "I've come to heal, deliver, recover, give liberty and preach the acceptable year of God".

Jesus came to give us these things! He came to look at everything that was broken in our lives and speak healing to it. He came to everything that was binding us to give us deliverance. He came to everything that we have lost and said, "I will recover it". Everything that has held us bound and kept us in jail He said, "I've come to give you liberty". This is our acceptable year of favor.

Psalm 102:13 says that the set time of favor has come. It goes on to say that this will be written for the generation to come. We are living in that time of set favor! Grace was never for us to continue in our stuff and in our sin. Grace through Jesus was so that we could be made free from it, not to live in it.

Today, get a great picture of the kingdom of God through this WIRED devotion. You are supposed to walk in freedom and in favor with the Lord Jesus. Everything that you have lost He said, "I've come to recover", especially that that had you lose your vision. This scripture is the job description of why Jesus came. You are so valuable to Him and His love is so great for you that He gave Himself for you to walk in His freedom! Shout these words out loud: I am free through Jesus Christ!

What did the words of Jesus speak to you today?

_____

_____

_____

_____

_____

How can you apply them to your life?

_____

_____

_____

_____

_____

Luke6
In a cornfield, on the Sabbath, to the Pharisees
3 Have ye not read so much as this, what David did, when himself was an hungred, and they which were with him; 4 how he went into the house of God, and did take and eat the shewbread, and gave also to them that were with him; which it is not lawful to eat but for the priests alone? 5 That the Son of man is Lord also of the Sabbath.

In the synagogue, on the Sabbath, to a man with a withered hand
8 Rise up, and stand forth in the midst.

To the scribes and Pharisees
9 I will ask you one thing; Is it lawful on the Sabbath days to do good, or to do evil? to save life, or to destroy it?

To the man with a withered hand
10 Stretch forth thy hand. And he did so: and his hand was restored whole as the other.

In a plain, to his disciples
20 Blessed be ye poor: for yours is the kingdom of God.
21 Blessed are ye that hunger now: for ye shall be filled. Blessed are ye that weep now: for ye shall laugh. 22 Blessed are ye, when men shall hate you, and when they shall separate you from their company, and shall reproach you, and cast out your name as evil, for the Son of man's sake. 23 Rejoice ye in that day, and leap for joy: for, behold, your reward is great in heaven: for in the like manner did their fathers unto the prophets. 24 But woe unto you that are rich! for ye have received your consolation. 25 Woe unto you that are full! for ye shall hunger. Woe unto you that laugh now! for ye shall mourn and weep. 26 Woe unto you, when all men shall speak well of you! for so did their fathers to the false prophets. 27 But I say unto you which hear, Love your enemies, do good to them which hate you, 28 bless them that curse you, and pray for them which despitefully use you. 29 And unto him that smiteth thee on the one cheek offer also the other; and him that taketh away thy cloak forbid not to take thy coat also. 30 Give to every man that asketh of thee; and of him that taketh away thy goods ask them not again. 31 And as ye would that men should do to you, do ye also to them likewise. 32 For if ye love them which love you, what thank have ye? For sinners also love those that love them. 33 And if ye do good to them which do good to you, what thank have ye? For sinners also do even the same. 34 And if ye lend to them of whom ye hope to receive, what thank have ye? For sinners also lend to sinners, to receive as much again. 35 But love ye your enemies, and do good, and lend, hoping for nothing again; and your reward shall be great, and ye shall be the children of the Highest: for he is kind unto the unthankful and to the evil. 36 Be ye therefore merciful, as your Father also is merciful. 37 Judge not, and ye shall not be judged: condemn not, and ye shall not be condemned: forgive, and ye shall be forgiven: 38 give, and it shall be given unto you; good measure, pressed down, and shaken together, and running over, shall men give into your bosom. For with the same measure that ye mete withal it shall be measured to you again. 39 Can the blind lead the blind? Shall they not both fall into the ditch? 40 The disciple is not above his master: but every one that is perfect shall be as his master. 41 And why beholdest thou the mote that is in thy brother's eye, but perceivest not the beam that is in thine own eye? 42 Either how canst thou say to thy brother, Brother, let me pull out the mote that is in thine eye, when thou thyself beholdest not the beam that is in thine own eye? Thou hypocrite, cast out first the beam out of thine own eye, and then shalt thou see clearly to pull out the mote that is in thy brother's eye. 43 For a good tree bringeth not forth corrupt fruit; neither doth a corrupt tree bring forth good fruit. 44 For every tree is known by his own fruit. For of thorns men do not gather figs, nor of a bramble bush gather they grapes. 45 A good man out of the good treasure of his heart bringeth

forth that which is good; and an evil man out of the evil treasure of his heart bringeth forth that which is evil: for of the abundance of the heart his mouth speaketh. 46 And why call ye me, Lord, Lord, and do not the things which I say? 47 Whosoever cometh to me, and heareth my sayings, and doeth them, I will shew you to whom he is like: 48 he is like a man which built an house, and digged deep, and laid the foundation on a rock: and when the flood arose, the stream beat vehemently upon that house, and could not shake it: for it was founded upon a rock. 49 But he that heareth, and doeth not, is like a man that without a foundation built an house upon the earth; against which the stream did beat vehemently, and immediately it fell; and the ruin of that house was great.

DEVOTION

Halfway Point! Don't Turn Back...Turn It Up!

We're exactly halfway through this devotion. Isn't it interesting on this very day, halfway through Luke 6:8 Jesus tells the man, "Rise up, and stand forth in the middle"? Just reading that gives you a Rhema moment!

Jesus made a man stretch out something that had been paralyzed. Why don't you do that now? You're halfway! People in aviation call this the PNR... the "point of no return". It's when they're over the ocean and they reach an invisible line that they only have enough fuel to either go forward or turn around and go back. Today, GO FORWARD! Stretch out that very thing that has been paralyzed in you! Sure, religious folk are going to stand around and say it can't be done. Moreover, they're going to tell you today's not the day! Just as they did in the day Jesus performed this miracle. Do you want what they want or do you want what Jesus wants for your life? If you want what Jesus wants, it's going to cost you nothing more than to believe! Aren't you excited? Aren't you thrilled that once you lay everything down and go forward, miracles wait for you?

There's so much more on this devotion today. Luke 6:20-49 says what life should look like for you when you follow Jesus' words plainly! Haters are not motivators...haters are our prayer assignments. Then He goes on to say that if you do all these things, verse 38 promises it will be given back to us good measure, pressed down, shaken together, and running over! Whatever we give it comes back to us. MY GOODNESS!! Please consider what you're giving in life. Maybe today's a day you might want to change what you're sowing physically, spiritually, mentally and financially. Jesus, Himself says you're going to reap it!! Today on this halfway point, change what you're giving! Decide to give, love, help sinners, love your enemies, pray for your enemies, show mercy, judge not, condemn not, forgive...the list goes on! Today, don't go back to old wineskins! MOVE FORWARD! This devotion today is packed full of how to live the good life. Digest every one of the scriptures in Luke 6 and you will be so blessed!

What did the words of Jesus speak to you today?

_____

_____

_____

_____

_____

How can you apply them to your life?

_____

_____

_____

_____

_____

Luke 7
In Capernaum, to the people that followed him, concerning the centurion
9 I say unto you, I have not found so great faith, no, not in Israel. 10 And they that were sent, returning to the house, found the servant whole that had been sick.

In Nain, to a widow
13 Weep not.

To the widow's dead son
14 Young man, I say unto thee, Arise. 15 And he that was dead sat up, and began to speak.

To two of John the Baptist's disciples
22 Go your way, and tell John what things ye have seen and heard; how that the blind see, the lame walk, the lepers are cleansed, the deaf hear, the dead are raised, to the poor the gospel is preached. 23 And blessed is he, whosoever shall not be offended in me.

To the people, concerning John the Baptist
24 What went ye out into the wilderness for to see? A reed shaken with the wind? 25 But what went ye out for to see? A man clothed in soft raiment? Behold, they which are gorgeously apparelled, and live delicately, are in kings' courts. 26 But what went ye out for to see? A prophet? Yea, I say unto you, and much more than a prophet. 27 This is he, of whom it is written, Behold, I send my messenger before thy face, which shall prepare thy way before thee. 28 For I say unto you, Among those that are born of women there is not a greater prophet than John the Baptist: but he that is least in the kingdom of God is greater than he.

To the Pharisees and lawyers
31 Whereunto then shall I liken the men of this generation? And to what are they like? 32 They are like unto children sitting in the marketplace, and calling one to another, and saying, We have piped unto you, and ye have not danced; we have mourned to you, and ye have not wept. 33 For John the Baptist came neither eating bread nor drinking wine; and ye say, He hath a devil. 34 The Son of man is come eating and drinking; and ye say, Behold a gluttonous man, and a winebibber, a friend of publicans and sinners! 35 But wisdom is justified of all her children.

In Simon's house, to Simon
40 Simon, I have somewhat to say unto thee. 41 There was a certain creditor which had two debtors: the one owed five hundred pence, and the other fifty. 42 And when they had nothing to pay, he frankly forgave them both. Tell me therefore, which of them will love him most? 43 Simon answered and said, I suppose that he, to whom he forgave most. Thou hast rightly judged. 44 Seest thou this woman? I entered into thine house, thou gavest me no water for my feet: but she hath washed my feet with tears, and wiped them with the hairs of her head. 45 Thou gavest me no kiss: but this woman since the time I came in hath not ceased to kiss my feet. 46 My head with oil thou didst not anoint: but this woman hath anointed my feet with ointment. 47 Wherefore I say unto thee, her sins, which are many, are forgiven; for she loved much: but to whom little is forgiven, the same loveth little.

To the woman
48 Thy sins are forgiven. 50 Thy faith hath saved thee; go in peace.

Luke 8
To many people
5 A sower went out to sow his seed: and as he sowed, some fell by the way side; and it was trodden down, and the fowls of the air devoured it. 6 And some fell upon a rock; and as soon as it was sprung up, it withered away, because it lacked moisture. 7 And some fell among thorns; and the thorns sprang up with it, and choked it. 8 And other fell on good ground, and sprang up, and bare fruit an hundredfold. He that hath ears to hear, let him hear.

To his disciples
10 Unto you it is given to know the mysteries of the kingdom of God: but to others in parables; that seeing they might not see, and hearing they might not understand. 11 Now the parable is this: The seed is the word of God. 12 Those by the way side are they that hear; then cometh the devil, and taketh away the word out of their hearts, lest they should believe and be saved. 13 They on the rock are they, which, when they hear, receive the word with joy; and these have no root, which for a while believe, and in time of temptation fall away. 14 And that which fell among thorns are they, which, when they have heard, go forth, and are choked with cares and riches and pleasures of this life, and bring no fruit to perfection. 15 But that on the good ground are they, which in an honest and good heart, having heard the word, keep it, and bring forth fruit with patience. 16 No man, when he hath lighted a candle, covereth it with a vessel, or putteth it under a bed; but setteth it on a candlestick, that they which enter in may see the light. 17 For nothing is secret, that shall not be made manifest; neither anything hid, that shall not be known and come abroad. 18 Take heed therefore how ye hear: for whosoever hath, to him shall be given; and whosoever hath not, from him shall be taken even that which he seemeth to have.

To certain people
21 My mother and my brethren are these which hear the word of God, and do it.

On a ship, to his disciples
22 Let us go over unto the other side of the lake.

After rebuking the storm, to his disciples
25 Where is your faith?

In the country of the Gadarenes, to the unclean spirit
30 What is thy name?

To the man out of whom the devils were departed
39 Return to thine own house, and shew how great things God hath done unto thee.

DEVOTION

Greater Than

Jesus speaks concerning John the Baptist and says something after he talks about how great John was. Jesus says, "There is none greater than the prophet John the Baptist: but he that is least in the kingdom of God is GREATER THAN he".

That will puzzle you until you realize what Jesus was saying. Let's put it this way:

Imagine on top of a mountain a huge boulder sitting there. It's the largest of all rocks. People travel from all over the world to see that rock because it is so huge on top of the mountain. But underneath the mountain is a diamond that is the size of a penny. Which is greater? What is extremely huge on top of the mountain or the small diamond inside the mountain? Without hesitation, the diamond is greater in value!

What Jesus is saying here is that John the Baptist represents the greatest of an old covenant, but after Jesus we receive a new covenant because the Bible says the Holy Spirit has been given to all of us. We now operate under a new covenant! Jesus said these words concerning John, "Among those that are born of women". This lets us know Jesus is talking about those who are least in the kingdom that are greater than John, are people that were born of women and of the Spirit. The Spirit of God dwells inside of all of us now because of the price Jesus paid. Pentecost was the birthing of a great church…US! The Spirit of God is living on the inside of the believer, doing the works of Jesus. You have a GREATER THAN anointing on your life. Choose to walk in that today. Be GREAT in Jesus!

What did the words of Jesus speak to you today?

_____
_____
_____
_____
_____

How can you apply them to your life?

_____
_____
_____
_____
_____

Luke 8
To the multitudes thronging and pressing him
45 Who touched me? 46 Somebody hath touched me: for I perceive that virtue is gone out of me.

To a woman having an issue of blood
48 Daughter, be of good comfort: thy faith hath made thee whole; go in peace.

To Jairus
50 Fear not: believe only, and she shall be made whole.

At Jairus' house, to those that wept
52 Weep not; she is not dead, but sleepeth.

To Jairus' daughter
54 Maid, arise.

Chapter 9
To his disciples
3 Take nothing for your journey, neither staves, nor scrip, neither bread, neither money; neither have two coats apiece. 4 And whatsoever house ye enter into, there abide, and thence depart. 5 And whosoever will not receive you, when ye go out of that city, shake off the very dust from your feet for a testimony against them.

In a desert place, to the disciples
13 Give ye them to eat. 14 Make them sit down by fifties in a company.

To his disciples
18 Whom say the people that I am? 20 But whom say ye that I am? 22 The Son of man must suffer many things, and be rejected of the elders and chief priests and scribes, and be slain, and be raised the third day. 23 If any man will come after me, let him deny himself, and take up his cross daily, and follow me. 24 For whosoever will save his life shall lose it: but whosoever will lose his life for my sake, the same shall save it. 25 For what is a man advantaged, if he gain the whole world, and lose himself, or be cast away? 26 For whosoever shall be ashamed of me and of my words, of him shall the Son of man be ashamed, when he shall come in his own glory, and in his Father's, and of the holy angels. 27 But I tell you of a truth, there be some standing here, which shall not taste of death, till they see the kingdom of God.

At the transfiguration of Jesus
The Father spoke
35 This is my beloved Son: hear him.

To the disciples and the father of a possessed son
41 O faithless and perverse generation, how long shall I be with you, and suffer you? Bring thy son hither.

To his disciples
44 Let these sayings sink down into your ears: for the Son of man shall be delivered into the hands of men. 48 Whosoever shall receive this child in my name receiveth me: and whosoever shall receive me receiveth him that sent me: for he that is least among you all, the same shall be great.

To John the Apostle
50 Forbid him not: for he that is not against us is for us.

In a village of the Samaritans, to James and John
55 Ye know not what manner of spirit ye are of. 56 For the Son of man is not come to destroy men's lives, but to save them.

To a certain man who said he would follow Jesus
58 Foxes have holes, and birds of the air have nests; but the Son of man hath not where to lay his head. To another man
59 Follow me .60 Let the dead bury their dead: but go thou and preach the kingdom of God.

To another man
62 No man, having put his hand to the plough, and looking back, is fit for the kingdom of God.

DEVOTION

Chiropractic Faith!

Luke 9:25...Very sobering words for those who have spent their whole life trying to gain the world. What if you climbed the mountain of life and realize you were on top of the wrong mountain at the end? That's what many people do. We choose "our will" over "His Will"! Many of you have asked, what if God's will is not mine? What if what He wants is not what I want?

Here is something we all need to know about God, He will never make you give something up that He doesn't have something better in store for you. For some of you reading this it may mean a whole complete life change. For others, just a minor adjustment.

Use this illustration concerning these words of Jesus: What if a man or a woman lived their whole life making great riches and a great name for themselves yet they were in miserable pain in their body? Everyone knew them and everyone wished that they had their money, but they did not realize that the pain this person was in was greater than the possessions they had. Then one day that person with great riches walks in a chiropractor's office and asks for an adjustment. They sit on the table and receive an adjustment in their back in the pain goes away. Their whole life was lived in pain when all they needed was one adjustment! Changing one thing puts things back in order. This is what Jesus is saying. Why would you live a life and gain everything in it while the whole time you lived in pain? He goes on to say that if you don't speak of Me or you are ashamed of Me, that on the great day, He will be ashamed to speak your name. Make a choice today. Choose Jesus! This passage of scripture does not say anything about having to be poor to follow Jesus. Jesus is simply saying give me everything you have and I'll give you everything I have. All it takes is one adjustment! CHOOSE JESUS!

What did the words of Jesus speak to you today?

_____

_____

_____

_____

_____

How can you apply them to your life?

_____

_____

_____

_____

_____

Luke 10
To the appointed seventy

2 The harvest truly is great, but the labourers are few: pray ye therefore the Lord of the harvest, that he would send forth labourers into his harvest. 3 Go your ways: behold, I send you forth as lambs among wolves. 4 Carry neither purse, nor scrip, nor shoes: and salute no man by the way. 5 And into whatsoever house ye enter, first say, Peace be to this house. 6 And if the son of peace be there, your peace shall rest upon it: if not, it shall turn to you again. 7 And in the same house remain, eating and drinking such things as they give: for the labourer is worthy of his hire. Go not from house to house. 8 And into whatsoever city ye enter, and they receive you, eat such things as are set before you: 9 and heal the sick that are therein, and say unto them, The kingdom of God is come nigh unto you. 10 But into whatsoever city ye enter, and they receive you not, go your ways out into the streets of the same, and say, 11 Even the very dust of your city, which cleaveth on us, we do wipe off against you: notwithstanding be ye sure of this, that the kingdom of God is come nigh unto you. 12 But I say unto you, that it shall be more tolerable in that day for Sodom, than for that city. 13 Woe unto thee, Chorazin! Woe unto thee, Bethsaida! For if the mighty works had been done in Tyre and Sidon, which have been done in you, they had a great while ago repented, sitting in sackcloth and ashes. 14 But it shall be more tolerable for Tyre and Sidon at the judgment, than for you. 15 And thou, Capernaum, which art exalted to heaven, shalt be thrust down to hell. 16 He that heareth you heareth me; and he that despiseth you despiseth me; and he that despiseth me despiseth him that sent me. 18 I beheld Satan as lightning fall from heaven. 19 Behold, I give unto you power to tread on serpents and scorpions, and over all the power of the enemy: and nothing shall by any means hurt you. 20 Notwithstanding in this rejoice not, that the spirits are subject unto you; but rather rejoice, because your names are written in heaven.

To his Father

21 I thank thee, O Father, Lord of heaven and earth, that thou hast hid these things from the wise and prudent, and hast revealed them unto babes: even so, Father; for so it seemed good in thy sight. 22 All things are delivered to me of my Father: and no man knoweth who the Son is, but the Father; and who the Father is, but the Son, and he to whom the Son will reveal him.

To his disciples

23 Blessed are the eyes which see the things that ye see:
24 for I tell you, that many prophets and kings have desired to see those things which ye see, and have not seen them; and to hear those things which ye hear, and have not heard them.

To a certain lawyer

26 What is written in the law? How readest thou?
28 Thou hast answered right: this do, and thou shalt live.
30 A certain man went down from Jerusalem to Jericho, and fell among thieves, which stripped him of his raiment, and wounded him, and departed, leaving him half dead. 31 And by chance there came down a certain priest that way: and when he saw him, he passed by on the other side. 32 And likewise a Levite, when he was at the place, came and looked on him, and passed by on the other side. 33 But a certain Samaritan, as he journeyed, came where he was: and when he saw him, he had compassion on him, 34 and went to him, and bound up his wounds, pouring in oil and wine, and set him on his own beast, and brought him to an inn, and took care of him. 35 And on the morrow when he departed, he took out two pence, and gave them to the host, and said unto him, Take care of him; and whatsoever thou spendest more, when I come again, I will repay thee. 36 Which now of these three, thinkest thou, was neighbour unto him that fell among the thieves?

37 Go, and do thou likewise.

In Mary and Martha's house, to Martha
41 Martha, Martha, thou art careful and troubled about many things: 42 but one thing is needful: and Mary hath chosen that good part, which shall not be taken away from her.

DEVOTION

For Hire!

Don't you love how this day begins? "The harvest is great", however the labourers are few.

Probably one of the most important things in business is supply and demand. What a horrible feeling for a business owner who has a great demand to fill for an order, however he has no supply. Probably the only thing worse is having too much supply and no demand! Having everything somebody needs yet nobody wants it! Or should we say nobody wants to work for it!

Jesus said at one point, "Every man presses his way into the kingdom". Whatever revelation that you received about the kingdom is where you will be in it! The kingdom of God must expand and it must grow, but it will take laborers to make that happen. There is a huge FOR HIRE sign that is constantly posted in the kingdom. People who will pick up the call, carry the cross, and do the will of God whether money is involved or not. We need great men and women of God who come with a price paid and not a price tag. We need women and men who know how to get their hands dirty and get in the gutters of life, to the broken and hurting, wanting to bring them in to the harvest!

One of the most derailing mindsets of evangelism is rejection! But Jesus says to us whatever city does not receive us, or family, or people, make sure to wipe the dust off and in one of the Gospels it says "let your peace return to you".

Today choose to be those who are on the wall praying to the Lord of the harvest for just one divine appointment today. Somebody to cross my path that I may expand the kingdom.

What did the words of Jesus speak to you today?

_____
_____
_____
_____
_____

How can you apply them to your life?

_____
_____
_____
_____
_____

Luke 11
In a certain place where he was praying, to his disciples
2 When ye pray, say, Our Father which art in heaven, Hallowed be thy name. Thy kingdom come. Thy will be done, as in heaven, so in earth. 3 Give us day by day our daily bread. 4 And forgive us our sins; for we also forgive every one that is indebted to us. And lead us not into temptation; but deliver us from evil. 5 Which of you shall have a friend, and shall go unto him at midnight, and say unto him, Friend, lend me three loaves; 6 for a friend of mine in his journey is come to me, and I have nothing to set before him? 7 And he from within shall answer and say, Trouble me not: the door is now shut, and my children are with me in bed; I cannot rise and give thee. 8 I say unto you, Though he will not rise and give him, because he is his friend, yet because of his importunity he will rise and give him as many as he needeth. 9 And I say unto you, Ask, and it shall be given you; seek, and ye shall find; knock, and it shall be opened unto you. 10 For every one that asketh receiveth; and he that seeketh findeth; and to him that knocketh it shall be opened. 11 If a son shall ask bread of any of you that is a father, will he give him a stone? Or if he ask a fish, will he for a fish give him a serpent? 12 Or if he shall ask an egg, will he offer him a scorpion? 13 If ye then, being evil, know how to give good gifts unto your children: how much more shall your heavenly Father give the Holy Spirit to them that ask him?

To those who accused Jesus of casting out devils through Beelzebub
17 Every kingdom divided against itself is brought to desolation; and a house divided against a house falleth. 18 If Satan also be divided against himself, how shall his kingdom stand? Because ye say that I cast out devils through Beelzebub. 19 And if I by Beelzebub cast out devils, by whom do your sons cast them out? Therefore shall they be your judges. 20 But if I with the finger of God cast out devils, no doubt the kingdom of God is come upon you. 21 When a strong man armed keepeth his palace, his goods are in peace: 22 but when a stronger than he shall come upon him, and overcome him, he taketh from him all his armour wherein he trusted, and divideth his spoils. 23 He that is not with me is against me: and he that gathereth not with me scattereth. 24 When the unclean spirit is gone out of a man, he walketh through dry places, seeking rest; and finding none, he saith, I will return unto my house whence I came out. 25 And when he cometh, he findeth it swept and garnished. 26 Then goeth he, and taketh to him seven other spirits more wicked than himself; and they enter in, and dwell there: and the last state of that man is worse than the first.

To a certain woman
28 Yea rather, blessed are they that hear the word of God, and keep it.

To the people
29 This is an evil generation: they seek a sign; and there shall no sign be given it, but the sign of Jonas the prophet. 30 For as Jonas was a sign unto the Ninevites, so shall also the Son of man be to this generation. 31 The queen of the south shall rise up in the judgment with the men of this generation, and condemn them: for she came from the utmost parts of the earth to hear the wisdom of Solomon; and, behold, a greater than Solomon is here. 32 The men of Nineve shall rise up in the judgment with this generation, and shall condemn it: for they repented at the preaching of Jonas; and, behold, a greater than Jonas is here. 33 No man, when he hath lighted a candle, putteth it in a secret place, neither under a bushel, but on a candlestick, that they which come in may see the light. 34 The light of the body is the eye: therefore when thine eye is single, thy whole body also is full of light; but when thine eye is evil, thy body also is full of darkness. 35 Take heed therefore that the light which is in thee be not darkness. 36 If thy whole body therefore be full of light, having no part dark, the whole shall be full of light, as when the bright shining of a candle doth give thee light.

To a certain Pharisee, with whom he was dining

39 Now do ye Pharisees make clean the outside of the cup and the platter; but your inward part is full of ravening and wickedness. 40 Ye fools, did not he that made that which is without make that which is within also? 41 But rather give alms of such things as ye have; and, behold, all things are clean unto you. 42 But woe unto you, Pharisees! For ye tithe mint and rue and all manner of herbs, and pass over judgment and the love of God: these ought ye to have done, and not to leave the other undone. 43 Woe unto you, Pharisees! for ye love the uppermost seats in the synagogues, and greetings in the markets. 44 Woe unto you, scribes and Pharisees, hypocrites! For ye are as graves which appear not, and the men that walk over them are not aware of them.

To the lawyers

46 Woe unto you also, ye lawyers! For ye lade men with burdens grievous to be borne, and ye yourselves touch not the burdens with one of your fingers. 47 Woe unto you! For ye build the sepulchres of the prophets, and your fathers killed them. 48 Truly ye bear witness that ye allow the deeds of your fathers: for they indeed killed them, and ye build their sepulchres. 49 Therefore also said the wisdom of God, I will send them prophets and apostles, and some of them they shall slay and persecute: 50 that the blood of all the prophets, which was shed from the foundation of the world, may be required of this generation; 51 from the blood of Abel unto the blood of Zacharias, which perished between the altar and the temple: verily I say unto you, It shall be required of this generation. 52 Woe unto you, lawyers! For ye have taken away the key of knowledge: ye entered not in yourselves, and them that were entering in ye hindered.

DEVOTION

No Vacancy

Often when we travel and get tired we will stop in a city that has multiple hotels to choose from. Sometimes when we get off an exit we will go to two or three hotels trying to find just 1 room, but because there's something going on, such as baseball tournament, a big convention etc., there will not be one room available. No doubt it's very frustrating as we are tired and need to get rest! We want you to understand that's how the enemy feels about you!

Once you've decided to give your life completely to Jesus, that unclean spirit leaves you and then looks for another place to rest. This means that every unclean spirit has to have a place to rest in order to function. That's pretty scary if you think about it. All demonic activity happens when they find rest inside a person! Wow! But the point of this is when you get a deliverance, that spirit that was on you or in you leaves you, but when it cannot find the rest, comes back to see if it can find rest in you again...after all, it knows you struggled before!!! If that spirit finds you not full of the word and full of God, yet you are nicely swept and clean, which simply means EMPTY, it will bring seven of its friends MORE wicked than itself.

PLEASE CLOSE THE DOOR TO ALL SPIRITS when you get saved and delivered! Don't allow yourself to fall back into the same stuff you dealt with before! Temptation is not a sin however, "lust conceived" is! Always remember just because you receive salvation doesn't mean your flesh won't crave bad things. Keep yourself full. Keep yourself plugged into a house of worship. Keep yourself in the mix of what is going on in your house. When the enemy comes in to your city make sure he knows there is NO VACANCY!

What did the words of Jesus speak to you today?

_____

_____

_____

_____

_____

How can you apply them to your life?

_____

_____

_____

_____

_____

Luke 12
To his disciples

1 Beware ye of the leaven of the Pharisees, which is hypocrisy. 2 For there is nothing covered, that shall not be revealed; neither hid, that shall not be known. 3 Therefore whatsoever ye have spoken in darkness shall be heard in the light; and that which ye have spoken in the ear in closets shall be proclaimed upon the housetops. 4 And I say unto you my friends, Be not afraid of them that kill the body, and after that have no more that they can do. 5 But I will forewarn you whom ye shall fear: Fear him, which after he hath killed hath power to cast into hell; yea, I say unto you, Fear him. 6 Are not five sparrows sold for two farthings, and not one of them is forgotten before God? 7 But even the very hairs of your head are all numbered. Fear not therefore: ye are of more value than many sparrows. 8 Also I say unto you, Whosoever shall confess me before men, him shall the Son of man also confess before the angels of God: 9 but he that denieth me before men shall be denied before the angels of God. 10 And whosoever shall speak a word against the Son of man, it shall be forgiven him: but unto him that blasphemeth against the Holy Ghost it shall not be forgiven. 11 And when they bring you unto the synagogues, and unto magistrates, and powers, take ye no thought how or what thing ye shall answer, or what ye shall say: 12 for the Holy Ghost shall teach you in the same hour what ye ought to say.

To one of the multitude
14 Man, who made me a judge or a divider over you?

To the multitude
15 Take heed, and beware of covetousness: for a man's life consisteth not in the abundance of the things which he possesseth. 16 And he spake a parable unto them, The ground of a certain rich man brought forth plentifully: 17 and he thought within himself, saying, What shall I do, because I have no room where to bestow my fruits? 18 And he said, This will I do: I will pull down my barns, and build greater; and there will I bestow all my fruits and my goods.
19 And I will say to my soul, Soul, thou hast much goods laid up for many years; take thine ease, eat, drink, and be merry. 20 But God said unto him, Thou fool, this night thy soul shall be required of thee: then whose shall those things be, which thou hast provided? 21 So is he that layeth up treasure for himself, and is not rich toward God.

To his disciples
22 Therefore I say unto you, Take no thought for your life, what ye shall eat; neither for the body, what ye shall put on. 23 The life is more than meat, and the body is more than raiment. 24 Consider the ravens: for they neither sow nor reap; which neither have storehouse nor barn; and God feedeth them: how much more are ye better than the fowls? 25 And which of you with taking thought can add to his stature one cubit? 26 If ye then be not able to do that thing which is least, why take ye thought for the rest? 27 Consider the lilies how they grow: they toil not, they spin not; and yet I say unto you, that Solomon in all his glory was not arrayed like one of these. 28 If then God so clothe the grass, which is to-day in the field, and to-morrow is cast into the oven; how much more will he clothe you, O ye of little faith? 29 And seek not ye what ye shall eat, or what ye shall drink, neither be ye of doubtful mind. 30 For all these things do the nations of the world seek after: and your Father knoweth that ye have need of these things. 31 But rather seek ye the kingdom of God; and all these things shall be added unto you. 32 Fear not, little flock; for it is your Father's good pleasure to give you the kingdom. 33 Sell that ye have, and give alms; provide yourselves bags which wax not old, a treasure in the heavens that faileth not, where no thief approacheth, neither moth corrupteth. 34 For where your treasure is, there will your heart be also. 35 Let your loins be girded about, and your lights burning; 36 and ye yourselves like unto men that wait for their lord, when he will return from the wedding; that when he cometh and knocketh, they may

open unto him immediately. 37 Blessed are those servants, whom the lord when he cometh shall find watching: verily I say unto you, that he shall gird himself, and make them to sit down to meat, and will come forth and serve them. 38 And if he shall come in the second watch, or come in the third watch, and find them so, blessed are those servants. 39 And this know, that if the good man of the house had known what hour the thief would come, he would have watched, and not have suffered his house to be broken through. 40 Be ye therefore ready also: for the Son of man cometh at an hour when ye think not.

To Peter and the people
42 Who then is that faithful and wise steward, whom his lord shall make ruler over his household, to give them their portion of meat in due season? 43 Blessed is that servant, whom his lord when he cometh shall find so doing. 44 Of a truth I say unto you, that he will make him ruler over all that he hath. 45 But and if that servant say in his heart, My lord delayeth his coming; and shall begin to beat the menservants and maidens, and to eat and drink, and to be drunken; 46 the lord of that servant will come in a day when he looketh not for him, and at an hour when he is not aware, and will cut him in sunder, and will appoint him his portion with the unbelievers. 47 And that servant, which knew his lord's will, and prepared not himself, neither did according to his will, shall be beaten with many stripes. 48 But he that knew not, and did commit things worthy of stripes, shall be beaten with few stripes. For unto whomsoever much is given, of him shall be much required: and to whom men have committed much, of him they will ask the more. 49 I am come to send fire on the earth; and what will I if it be already kindled? 50 But I have a baptism to be baptized with; and how am I straitened till it be accomplished! 51 Suppose ye that I am come to give peace on earth? I tell you, Nay; but rather division: 52 for from henceforth there shall be five in one house divided, three against two, and two against three. 53 The father shall be divided against the son, and the son against the father; the mother against the daughter, and the daughter against the mother; the mother in law against her daughter in law, and the daughter in law against her mother in law.

To the people
54 When ye see a cloud rise out of the west, straightway ye say, There cometh a shower; and so it is. 55 And when ye see the south wind blow, ye say, There will be heat; and it cometh to pass. 56 Ye hypocrites, ye can discern the face of the sky and of the earth; but how is it that ye do not discern this time? 57 Yea, and why even of yourselves judge ye not what is right? 58 When thou goest with thine adversary to the magistrate, as thou art in the way, give diligence that thou mayest be delivered from him; lest he hale thee to the judge, and the judge deliver thee to the officer, and the officer cast thee into prison. 59 I tell thee, thou shalt not depart thence, till thou hast paid the very last mite.

DEVOTION

Unforgivable Sin...Forever Damned?

For this devotion we want to take time to explain what the unpardonable sin really is. Since the Bible says in 1 John 1:9, "If we confess our sins, He is faithful and just and will forgive us our sins and purify us from all unrighteousness...", how can there be an unforgivable sin? Since we are reading this in context, He's talking concerning the leaven of the Pharisees who are constantly denying that He is the Son of God. Jesus says to His disciples that these Pharisees constantly deny Me, the Holy Spirit's conviction to repent and be saved. Blaspheming the Holy Spirit simply means rejecting the conviction over and over and over. It's one thing to be miserable with conviction, it's a whole other thing to live a life void of it. It's an automatic forever damnation. To know better yet to continue in your folly and sin, repeatedly pushing away the conviction of the Holy Spirit.

Remember this if you are already saved, there are certain people in your life that just don't want to change no matter what! Your job is to do the same thing that Jesus told His disciples…continue to speak with the Holy Spirit and continue to be that light in front of them. It is not your job to play the role of the Holy Spirit. That's not your role! As long as you are being that light, relieve yourself of feeling responsible.

What did the words of Jesus speak to you today?

_____
_____
_____
_____
_____

How can you apply them to your life?

_____
_____
_____
_____
_____

Luke 13

To some who told him of the Galilaeans, whose blood Pilate had mingled with their sacrifices
2 Suppose ye that these Galilaeans were sinners above all the Galilaeans, because they suffered such things? 3 I tell you, Nay: but, except ye repent, ye shall all likewise perish. 4 Or those eighteen, upon whom the tower in Siloam fell, and slew them, think ye that they were sinners above all men that dwelt in Jerusalem? 5 I tell you, Nay: but, except ye repent, ye shall all likewise perish. 6 He spake also this parable; A certain man had a fig tree planted in his vineyard; and he came and sought fruit thereon, and found none. 7 Then said he unto the dresser of his vineyard, Behold, these three years I come seeking fruit on this fig tree, and find none: cut it down; why cumbereth it the ground? 8 And he answering said unto him, Lord, let it alone this year also, till I shall dig about it, and dung it: 9 and if it bear fruit, well: and if not, then after that thou shalt cut it down.

In the synagogue, on the Sabbath, to a woman which had a spirit of infirmity

12 Woman, thou art loosed from thine infirmity. 13 And he laid his hands on her: and immediately she was made straight, and glorified God.

To the ruler of the synagogue

15 Thou hypocrite, doth not each one of you on the Sabbath loose his ox or his ass from the stall, and lead him away to watering? 16 And ought not this woman, being a daughter of Abraham, whom Satan hath bound, lo, these eighteen years, be loosed from this bond on the Sabbath day?

To the people

18 Unto what is the kingdom of God like? And whereunto shall I resemble it? 19 It is like a grain of mustard seed, which a man took, and cast into his garden; and it grew, and waxed a great tree; and the fowls of the air lodged in the branches of it. 20 Whereunto shall I liken the kingdom of God? 21 It is like leaven, which a woman took and hid in three measures of meal, till the whole was leavened.

To one that journeyed with him toward Jerusalem

24 Strive to enter in at the strait gate: for many, I say unto you, will seek to enter in, and shall not be able. 25 When once the master of the house is risen up, and hath shut to the door, and ye begin to stand without, and to knock at the door, saying, Lord, Lord, open unto us; and he shall answer and say unto you, I know you not whence ye are: 26 then shall ye begin to say, We have eaten and drunk in thy presence, and thou hast taught in our streets. 27 But he shall say, I tell you, I know you not whence ye are; depart from me, all ye workers of iniquity. 28 There shall be weeping and gnashing of teeth, when ye shall see Abraham, and Isaac, and Jacob, and all the prophets, in the kingdom of God, and you yourselves thrust out. 29 And they shall come from the east, and from the west, and from the north, and from the south, and shall sit down in the kingdom of God. 30 And, behold, there are last which shall be first, and there are first which shall be last.

To certain of the Pharisees, who told him Herod would kill him

32 Go ye, and tell that fox, Behold, I cast out devils, and I do cures to-day and to-morrow, and the third day I shall be perfected. 33 Nevertheless I must walk to-day, and to-morrow, and the day following: for it cannot be that a prophet perish out of Jerusalem. 34 O Jerusalem, Jerusalem, which killest the prophets, and stonest them that are sent unto thee; how often would I have gathered thy children together, as a hen doth gather her brood under her wings, and ye would not! 35 Behold, your house is left unto you desolate: and verily I say unto you, Ye shall not see me, until the time come when ye shall say, Blessed is he that cometh in the name of the Lord.

DEVOTION

Your Enemy Has to Agree with Your Blessings

Jesus says in Luke 13:18 what the kingdom of God looks like! He says it's like a grain of mustard seed and when it grew up the birds lodged in the branches.

Whenever you scatter seed on the ground the first thing that happens is the birds gather to eat the seeds. Often people will cover the seed with hay or straw to try to keep the birds away and some people will even go out and shew them away. In the parable of the sower, we find out that the birds represented Satan, immediately snatching away the seed.

The beautiful thing about the mustard seed parable is not the size of the seed, rather the conviction of it. The mustard seed does not fall into the ground and change its mind that it wants to be an apple tree. No, however it knows what it's supposed to produce when it is covered up with dirt, when it is trying to break through, when the rain hits it, when the lightning strikes, when the storms blow…it holds fast to the fact that it was created to produce what a mustard seed produces!!

When you realize what this word of God does to you in the words of Jesus and you get that conviction inside of you that this word belongs to you, no matter what happens to you in life, it cannot take away the seed that has been planted. The enemy who wants to take away that seed will eventually have to park himself on your branches! In other words, the enemy has to agree with your blessings. He will realize, as well as you will realize, that even though you were once small, you held fast that you were planted in the kingdom!

Today, go ahead and speak it out loud that you're going to remain planted! What God started in you, He will finish and you will eventually grow something so great that even the enemy will have to publicly recognize the greatness in you which is the Holy Spirit!

What did the words of Jesus speak to you today?

_____
_____
_____
_____
_____

How can you apply them to your life?

_____
_____
_____
_____
_____

Luke 14
In the house of one of the chief Pharisees, to the lawyers and Pharisees
3 Is it lawful to heal on the Sabbath day? 5 Which of you shall have an ass or an ox fallen into a pit, and will not straightway pull him out on the Sabbath day?

To those which were bidden
8 When thou art bidden of any man to a wedding, sit not down in the highest room; lest a more honourable man than thou be bidden of him; 9 and he that bade thee and him come and say to thee, Give this man place; and thou begin with shame to take the lowest room. 10 But when thou art bidden, go and sit down in the lowest room; that when he that bade thee cometh, he may say unto thee, Friend, go up higher: then shalt thou have worship in the presence of them that sit at meat with thee.
11 For whosoever exalteth himself shall be abased; and he that humbleth himself shall be exalted.

To him that bade him
12 When thou makest a dinner or a supper, call not thy friends, nor thy brethren, neither thy kinsmen, nor thy rich neighbours; lest they also bid thee again, and a recompence be made thee. 13 But when thou makest a feast, call the poor, the maimed, the lame, the blind: 14 and thou shalt be blessed; for they cannot recompense thee: for thou shalt be recompensed at the resurrection of the just.

To one of them that sat at meat with him
16 A certain man made a great supper, and bade many: 17 and sent his servant at supper time to say to them that were bidden, Come; for all things are now ready. 18 And they all with one consent began to make excuse. The first said unto him, I have bought a piece of ground, and I must needs go and see it: I pray thee have me excused. 19 And another said, I have bought five yoke of oxen, and I go to prove them: I pray thee have me excused. 20 And another said, I have married a wife, and therefore I cannot come. 21 So that servant came, and shewed his lord these things. Then the master of the house being angry said to his servant, Go out quickly into the streets and lanes of the city, and bring in hither the poor, and the maimed, and the halt, and the blind. 22 And the servant said, Lord, it is done as thou hast commanded, and yet there is room. 23 And the lord said unto the servant, Go out into the highways and hedges, and compel them to come in, that my house may be filled.
24 For I say unto you, That none of those men which were bidden shall taste of my supper.

To great multitudes
26 If any man come to me, and hate not his father, and mother, and wife, and children, and brethren, and sisters, yea, and his own life also, he cannot be my disciple. 27 And whosoever doth not bear his cross, and come after me, cannot be my disciple. 28 For which of you, intending to build a tower, sitteth not down first, and counteth the cost, whether he have sufficient to finish it? 29 Lest haply, after he hath laid the foundation, and is not able to finish it, all that behold it begin to mock him, 30 saying, This man began to build, and was not able to finish. 31 Or what king, going to make war against another king, sitteth not down first, and consulteth whether he be able with ten thousand to meet him that cometh against him with twenty thousand? 32 Or else, while the other is yet a great way off, he sendeth an ambassage, and desireth conditions of peace.
33 So likewise, whosoever he be of you that forsaketh not all that he hath, he cannot be my disciple.
34 Salt is good: but if the salt have lost his savour, wherewith shall it be seasoned?
35 It is neither fit for the land, nor yet for the dunghill; but men cast it out. He that hath ears to hear, let him hear.

Luke 15
To the Pharisees and scribes

3 And he spake this parable unto them, 4 What man of you, having an hundred sheep, if he lose one of them, doth not leave the ninety and nine in the wilderness, and go after that which is lost, until he find it? 5 And when he hath found it, he layeth it on his shoulders, rejoicing. 6 And when he cometh home, he calleth together his friends and neighbours, saying unto them, Rejoice with me; for I have found my sheep which was lost. 7 I say unto you, that likewise joy shall be in heaven over one sinner that repenteth, more than over ninety and nine just persons, which need no repentance. 8 Either what woman having ten pieces of silver, if she lose one piece, doth not light a candle, and sweep the house, and seek diligently till she find it? 9 And when she hath found it, she calleth her friends and her neighbours together, saying, Rejoice with me; for I have found the piece which I had lost. 10 Likewise, I say unto you, there is joy in the presence of the angels of God over one sinner that repenteth. 11 A certain man had two sons: 12 and the younger of them said to his father, Father, give me the portion of goods that falleth to me. And he divided unto them his living. 13 And not many days after the younger son gathered all together, and took his journey into a far country, and there wasted his substance with riotous living. 14 And when he had spent all, there arose a mighty famine in that land; and he began to be in want. 15 And he went and joined himself to a citizen of that country; and he sent him into his fields to feed swine. 16 And he would fain have filled his belly with the husks that the swine did eat: and no man gave unto him. 17 And when he came to himself, he said, How many hired servants of my father's have bread enough and to spare, and I perish with hunger! 18 I will arise and go to my father, and will say unto him, Father, I have sinned against heaven, and before thee, 19 and am no more worthy to be called thy son: make me as one of thy hired servants. 20 And he arose, and came to his father. But when he was yet a great way off, his father saw him, and had compassion, and ran, and fell on his neck, and kissed him. 21 And the son said unto him, Father, I have sinned against heaven, and in thy sight, and am no more worthy to be called thy son. 22 But the father said to his servants, Bring forth the best robe, and put it on him; and put a ring on his hand, and shoes on his feet: 23 and bring hither the fatted calf, and kill it; and let us eat, and be merry: 24 for this my son was dead, and is alive again; he was lost, and is found. And they began to be merry. 25 Now his elder son was in the field: and as he came and drew nigh to the house, he heard music and dancing. 26 And he called one of the servants, and asked what these things meant. 27 And he said unto him, Thy brother is come; and thy father hath killed the fatted calf, because he hath received him safe and sound. 28 And he was angry, and would not go in: therefore came his father out, and intreated him. 29 And he answering said to his father, Lo, these many years do I serve thee, neither transgressed I at any time thy commandment: and yet thou never gavest me a kid, that I might make merry with my friends: 30 but as soon as this thy son was come, which hath devoured thy living with harlots, thou hast killed for him the fatted calf. 31 And he said unto him, Son, thou art ever with me, and all that I have is thine. 32 It was meet that we should make merry, and be glad: for this thy brother was dead, and is alive again; and was lost, and is found.

DEVOTION

The Great Supper

A few years ago we did something at our church called "THE GREAT SUPPER." We literally did what the scripture talked about. We set up the house of God with a huge table and had everybody in the church dress up in a five-star way, black pants, white shirt, black tie and shiny shoes. We then invited everybody we knew that was less fortunate and probably never had something like what we were about to do. We had chefs and cooks and servers and a decorating committee that made the place look like a white tablecloth restaurant! Homeless began to come that night and there was still room at the table. We took a broken down bus and went to a shelter and picked up another 20 or so people. What an incredible night it was as people in our church used their gifts and talents to entertain and worship in front of them. We got to know them, hear their stories, some good, some not so good, and some you didn't know if they were telling the truth or not but it really didn't matter. They were in our house and they were our guests.

If you really want to feel the same way Jesus felt, don't invite just the people that you're expecting to receive something from to your house. Invite somebody that you have seen that has never experienced what you have already. It's the same way in the spirit. Every day you see people that you know. They may look good on the outside but on the inside, they have never experienced the joy, peace, love and so much more that you have. I believe this great supper parable has more to do with us giving love to people that need it the most.

If we are always giving to people that we know we're going to get something back from, that's called investment and opportunity. Jesus nails it on the head right here that in His kingdom everybody gets a piece of the action, everybody is deserving, no matter if they can give back or not. We challenge you today to go bless somebody. It does not have to be money, it may be a 20 minute conversation with somebody who no one ever listens to. Go bless somebody right now and make it a point today to do this.

What did the words of Jesus speak to you today?

_____

_____

_____

_____

_____

How can you apply them to your life?

_____

_____

_____

_____

_____

Luke 16
To his disciples
1 There was a certain rich man, which had a steward; and the same was accused unto him that he had wasted his goods. 2 And he called him, and said unto him, How is it that I hear this of thee? Give an account of thy stewardship; for thou mayest be no longer steward. 3 Then the steward said within himself, What shall I do? For my lord taketh away from me the stewardship: I cannot dig; to beg I am ashamed. 4 I am resolved what to do, that, when I am put out of the stewardship, they may receive me into their houses. 5 So he called every one of his lord's debtors unto him, and said unto the first, How much owest thou unto my lord? 6 And he said, An hundred measures of oil. And he said unto him, Take thy bill, and sit down quickly, and write fifty. 7 Then said he to another, And how much owest thou? And he said, An hundred measures of wheat. And he said unto him, Take thy bill, and write fourscore. 8 And the lord commended the unjust steward, because he had done wisely: for the children of this world are in their generation wiser than the children of light. 9 And I say unto you, Make to yourselves friends of the mammon of unrighteousness; that, when ye fail, they may receive you into everlasting habitations. 10 He that is faithful in that which is least is faithful also in much: and he that is unjust in the least is unjust also in much. 11 If therefore ye have not been faithful in the unrighteous mammon, who will commit to your trust the true riches? 12 And if ye have not been faithful in that which is another man's, who shall give you that which is your own? 13 No servant can serve two masters: for either he will hate the one, and love the other; or else he will hold to the one, and despise the other. Ye cannot serve God and mammon.

To the Pharisees
15 Ye are they which justify yourselves before men; but God knoweth your hearts: for that which is highly esteemed among men is abomination in the sight of God. 16 The law and the prophets were until John: since that time the kingdom of God is preached, and every man presseth into it.17 And it is easier for heaven and earth to pass, than one tittle of the law to fail. 18 Whosoever putteth away his wife, and marrieth another, committeth adultery: and whosoever marrieth her that is put away from her husband committeth adultery.19 There was a certain rich man, which was clothed in purple and fine linen, and fared sumptuously every day: 20 and there was a certain beggar named Lazarus, which was laid at his gate, full of sores, 21 and desiring to be fed with the crumbs which fell from the rich man's table: moreover the dogs came and licked his sores. 22 And it came to pass, that the beggar died, and was carried by the angels into Abraham's bosom: the rich man also died, and was buried; 23 and in hell he lift up his eyes, being in torments, and seeth Abraham afar off, and Lazarus in his bosom. 24 And he cried and said, Father Abraham, have mercy on me, and send Lazarus, that he may dip the tip of his finger in water, and cool my tongue; for I am tormented in this flame. 25 But Abraham said, Son, remember that thou in thy lifetime receivedst thy good things, and likewise Lazarus evil things: but now he is comforted, and thou art tormented. 26 And beside all this, between us and you there is a great gulf fixed: so that they which would pass from hence to you cannot; neither can they pass to us that would come from thence.27 Then he said, I pray thee therefore, father, that thou wouldest send him to my father's house: 28 for I have five brethren; that he may testify unto them, lest they also come into this place of torment. 29 Abraham saith unto him, They have Moses and the prophets; let them hear them. 30 And he said, Nay, father Abraham: but if one went unto them from the dead, they will repent. 31 And he said unto him, If they hear not Moses and the prophets, neither will they be persuaded, though one rose from the dead.

DEVOTION

True Riches

God begins to speak to His disciples about stewardship. Two major words in the Bible Jesus talks about being a steward of…our time and our money. Jesus begins to tell His disciples to pay attention to how worldly people work with their "unrighteous mammon" or their money. The emphasis is not on how they should pay attention to the dishonest acts of the steward, rather how he works to steward what he had done wrong to his employer.

Jesus says how can we be trusted with the true riches if we don't know how to handle unrighteous mammon? He also says if we're not faithful with somebody else's here on earth, how can we ever expect to be given something of our own?

This is such a huge principle in the kingdom…being faithful with someone else's property or goods. Yes, it really is important what you do when no one is looking because you will give account for it one day. Even taking a few dollars from the cash register to go and get lunch because you feel like you deserve it. Sure, your employer may not catch you but the Lord takes note of it. The point is good stewardship should always bless the kingdom and not take from it! What we do on earth should depict the same. But Jesus gives a strong warning at the end to His disciples to not love money over God. This will take away the TRUE RICHES in your life. True riches are the spiritual blessings that you received through grace, peace, joy and so much more.

Today, make a decision to be wise with everything that you are entrusted with. Here's the big news: nothing on this earth really belongs to you even if your name's on the title or the deed. It's simply something God has blessed you with to use to bless the kingdom.

What did the words of Jesus speak to you today?

_____

_____

_____

_____

_____

How can you apply them to your life?

_____

_____

_____

_____

_____

Luke 17
To the disciples

1 It is impossible but that offences will come: but woe unto him, through whom they come! 2 It were better for him that a millstone were hanged about his neck, and he cast into the sea, than that he should offend one of these little ones. 3 Take heed to yourselves: If thy brother trespass against thee, rebuke him; and if he repent, forgive him. 4 And if he trespass against thee seven times in a day, and seven times in a day turn again to thee, saying, I repent; thou shalt forgive him. 6 If ye had faith as a grain of mustard seed, ye might say unto this sycamine tree, Be thou plucked up by the root, and be thou planted in the sea; and it should obey you. 7 But which of you, having a servant plowing or feeding cattle, will say unto him by and by, when he is come from the field, Go and sit down to meat? 8 And will not rather say unto him, Make ready wherewith I may sup, and gird thyself, and serve me, till I have eaten and drunken; and afterward thou shalt eat and drink? 9 Doth he thank that servant because he did the things that were commanded him? I trow not. 10 So likewise ye, when ye shall have done all those things which are commanded you, say, We are unprofitable servants: we have done that which was our duty to do.

In the midst of Samaria and Galilee, to ten lepers

14 Go shew yourselves unto the priests.

To the one thankful leper

17 Were there not ten cleansed? But where are the nine?
18 There are not found that returned to give glory to God, save this stranger. 19 Arise, go thy way: thy faith hath made thee whole.

To the Pharisees

20 The kingdom of God cometh not with observation: 21 neither shall they say, Lo here! Or, lo there! For, behold, the kingdom of God is within you.

To the disciples

22 The days will come, when ye shall desire to see one of the days of the Son of man, and ye shall not see it. 23 And they shall say to you, See here; or, see there: go not after them, nor follow them. 24 For as the lightning, that lighteneth out of the one part under heaven, shineth unto the other part under heaven; so shall also the Son of man be in his day. 25 But first must he suffer many things, and be rejected of this generation. 26 And as it was in the days of Noe, so shall it be also in the days of the Son of man. 27 They did eat, they drank, they married wives, they were given in marriage, until the day that Noe entered into the ark, and the flood came, and destroyed them all. 28 Likewise also as it was in the days of Lot; they did eat, they drank, they bought, they sold, they planted, they builded; 29 but the same day that Lot went out of Sodom it rained fire and brimstone from heaven, and destroyed them all. 30 Even thus shall it be in the day when the Son of man is revealed. 31 In that day, he which shall be upon the housetop, and his stuff in the house, let him not come down to take it away: and he that is in the field, let him likewise not return back. 32 Remember Lot's wife. 33 Whosoever shall seek to save his life shall lose it; and whosoever shall lose his life shall preserve it. 34 I tell you, in that night there shall be two men in one bed; the one shall be taken, and the other shall be left. 35 Two women shall be grinding together; the one shall be taken, and the other left. 36 Two men shall be in the field; the one shall be taken, and the other left. 37 Wheresoever the body is, thither will the eagles be gathered together.

Luke 18

1 And he spake a parable unto them to this end, that men ought always to pray, and not to faint; 2 There was in a city a judge, which feared not God, neither regarded man: 3 and there was a widow in that city; and she came unto him, saying, Avenge me of mine adversary. 4 And he would not for a while: but afterward he said within himself, Though I fear not God, nor regard man; 5 yet because this widow troubleth me, I will avenge her, lest by her continual coming she weary me. 6 Hear what the unjust judge saith. 7 And shall not God avenge his own elect, which cry day and night unto him, though he bear long with them? 8 I tell you that he will avenge them speedily. Nevertheless when the Son of man cometh, shall he find faith on the earth? 9 And he spake this parable unto certain which trusted in themselves that they were righteous, and despised others: 10 Two men went up into the temple to pray; the one a Pharisee, and the other a publican. 11 The Pharisee stood and prayed thus with himself, God, I thank thee, that I am not as other men are, extortioners, unjust, adulterers, or even as this publican. 12 I fast twice in the week, I give tithes of all that I possess. 13 And the publican, standing afar off, would not lift up so much as his eyes unto heaven, but smote upon his breast, saying, God be merciful to me a sinner. 14 I tell you, this man went down to his house justified rather than the other: for every one that exalteth himself shall be abased; and he that humbleth himself shall be exalted.

To his disciples
16 Suffer little children to come unto me, and forbid them not: for of such is the kingdom of God. 17 Verily I say unto you, Whosoever shall not receive the kingdom of God as a little child shall in no wise enter therein. 18 And a certain ruler asked him, saying, Good Master, what shall I do to inherit eternal life? 19 Why callest thou me good? None is good, save one, that is, God. 20 Thou knowest the commandments, Do not commit adultery, Do not kill, Do not steal, Do not bear false witness, Honour thy father and thy mother. 22 Yet lackest thou one thing: sell all that thou hast, and distribute unto the poor, and thou shalt have treasure in heaven: and come, follow me. 24 How hardly shall they that have riches enter into the kingdom of God! 25 For it is easier for a camel to go through a needle's eye, than for a rich man to enter into the kingdom of God.

To those who asked "Who then can be saved?"
27 The things which are impossible with men are possible with God.

To his disciples
29 Verily I say unto you, There is no man that hath left house, or parents, or brethren, or wife, or children, for the kingdom of God's sake, 30 who shall not receive manifold more in this present time, and in the world to come life everlasting.

To the twelve
31 Behold, we go up to Jerusalem, and all things that are written by the prophets concerning the Son of man shall be accomplished. 32 For he shall be delivered unto the Gentiles, and shall be mocked, and spitefully entreated, and spitted on: 33 and they shall scourge him, and put him to death: and the third day he shall rise again.

Near Jericho, to a blind man
41 What wilt thou that I shall do unto thee? 42 Receive thy sight: thy faith hath saved thee.

DEVOTION

Healed or Whole?

Jesus healed 10 lepers in Luke 17. All 10 walked away healed, I'm sure headed home to tell family that they have not been able to hug for years because of the leprosy. Walking through the streets proudly showing everybody that they are no longer enslaved with their sin. But only one comes back? And he is a stranger. He came back to give glory to God. There is power that will change your life through giving God some praise. Jesus said to the one that came back and was thankful, arise for your faith has made you WHOLE!

Nine were healed but one was made whole. Please understand that you can be healed in your body but not whole in your mind. These two words are completely different in the Greek. Healed represents a body cleansing. It literally says to remove impurities. However, the word "whole" is *sozo*, which means salvation. Salvation is a regenerative word, meaning born again...made new! God is not only a God that will recover you but He will restore you. A lot of people just want Him to get them out of a mess, but He wants more for us than just getting us out of our stuff. He wants to restore back to us what rightfully belongs to us. It is important to see that the man came back and praised, gave thanks to God! Nowhere in the Bible do I see that Jesus told us to remain quiet! It's actually quite opposite. Not trying to kill sacred cows or offend you, but when is the last time you gave God a TRUE PRAISE? A grateful praise, not attached to a need, just a simple, "God I thank you!!! Don't need anything, just thank you!"?

Today remember that God doesn't only want to recover you from sin but He wants to restore you! Make you new!

What did the words of Jesus speak to you today?

_____

_____

_____

_____

_____

How can you apply them to your life?

_____

_____

_____

_____

_____

In Jericho, to Zacchaeus
Luke 19
5 Zacchaeus, make haste, and come down; for to-day I must abide at thy house. 9 This day is salvation come to this house, forsomuch as he also is a son of Abraham. 10 For the Son of man is come to seek and to save that which was lost.

To those that thought the kingdom of God should immediately appear
12 A certain nobleman went into a far country to receive for himself a kingdom, and to return. 13 And he called his ten servants, and delivered them ten pounds, and said unto them, Occupy till I come. 14 But his citizens hated him, and sent a message after him, saying, We will not have this man to reign over us. 15 And it came to pass, that when he was returned, having received the kingdom, then he commanded these servants to be called unto him, to whom he had given the money, that he might know how much every man had gained by trading. 16 Then came the first, saying, Lord, thy pound hath gained ten pounds. 17 And he said unto him, Well, thou good servant: because thou hast been faithful in a very little, have thou authority over ten cities. 18 And the second came, saying, Lord, thy pound hath gained five pounds. 19 And he said likewise to him, Be thou also over five cities. 20 And another came, saying, Lord, behold, here is thy pound, which I have kept laid up in a napkin:21 for I feared thee, because thou art an austere man: thou takest up that thou layedst not down, and reapest that thou didst not sow. 22 And he saith unto him, Out of thine own mouth will I judge thee, thou wicked servant. Thou knewest that I was an austere man, taking up that I laid not down, and reaping that I did not sow:
23 wherefore then gavest not thou my money into the bank, that at my coming I might have required mine own with usury? 24 And he said unto them that stood by, Take from him the pound, and give it to him that hath ten pounds. 25 (And they said unto him, Lord, he hath ten pounds.) 26 For I say unto you, That unto every one which hath shall be given; and from him that hath not, even that he hath shall be taken away from him. 27 But those mine enemies, which would not that I should reign over them, bring hither, and slay them before me.

At the Mount of Olives, to two of his disciples
30 Go ye into the village over against you; in the which at your entering ye shall find a colt tied, whereon yet never man sat: loose him, and bring him hither.31 And if any man ask you, Why do ye loose him? Thus shall ye say unto him, Because the Lord hath need of him.

At the base of the Mount of Olives, to the Pharisees
40 I tell you that, if these should hold their peace, the stones would immediately cry out.

As he beheld Jerusalem
42 If thou hadst known, even thou, at least in this thy day, the things which belong unto thy peace! But now they are hid from thine eyes. 43 For the days shall come upon thee, that thine enemies shall cast a trench about thee, and compass thee round, and keep thee in on every side, 44 and shall lay thee even with the ground, and thy children within thee; and they shall not leave in thee one stone upon another; because thou knewest not the time of thy visitation.

In Jerusalem's temple, to them that sold therein
46 It is written, My house is the house of prayer: but ye have made it a den of thieves.

DEVOTION

Reaping the Rewards of Good Stewardship

Again, Jesus brings into consideration the importance of our stewardship. He begins to tell a parable about the man who left three servants in charge of his kingdom. He gave all three 10 pounds. He then says "occupy" until I come! Occupy means to possess, make profit, employ and invest. But here's the kicker that makes the whole story make sense, Jesus says in verse 26, "Everyone which has it shall be given and everyone who has not it shall be taken away". What is he talking about? They all had 10 pounds so he can't be talking about that. No, He is talking about revelation! Not the last book, He's talking about revelation in the mind! He who "gets this revelation" and works this revelation will always get more.

In all you're getting, get understanding and then put it in practice. Don't be one of those who live in Christ for 20 years but only have 1 year experienced 20 times over! GROW, GROW, GROW every year in Christ. Every day receive new revelation, new understanding and become empowered to grow the kingdom of God. God will come back and ask you what did you do with what I gave you and on that day, you're going to want to say you've been faithful with the gifts, talent, money that He gave to you! You can only reap from whatever level of revelation you have...30,60 or 100-fold!

What did the words of Jesus speak to you today?

_____

_____

_____

_____

_____

How can you apply them to your life?

_____

_____

_____

_____

_____

Luke 20
In Jerusalem's temple, to the chief priests and the scribes, with the elders
3 I will also ask you one thing; and answer me: 4 The baptism of John, was it from heaven, or of men? 8 Neither tell I you by what authority I do these things. 9 Then began He to speak to the people this parable; "A certain man planted a vineyard, and let it forth to husbandmen, and went into a far country for a long time. 10 And at the season he sent a servant to the husbandmen, that they should give him of the fruit of the vineyard: but the husbandmen beat him, and sent him away empty. 11 And again he sent another servant: and they beat him also, and entreated him shamefully, and sent him away empty. 12 And again he sent a third: and they wounded him also, and cast him out. 13Then said the lord of the vineyard, What shall I do? I will send my beloved son: it may be they will reverence him when they see him. 14 But when the husbandmen saw him, they reasoned among themselves, saying, this is the heir: come, let us kill him, that the inheritance may be ours. 15 So they cast him out of the vineyard, and killed him. What therefore shall the lord of the vineyard do unto them? 16 He shall come and destroy these husbandmen, and shall give the vineyard to others. 17 What is this then that is written, the stone which the builders rejected, the same is become the head of the corner? 18 Whosoever shall fall upon that stone shall be broken; but on whomsoever it shall fall, it will grind him to powder.

To the chief priests and scribes
23 Why tempt ye me? 24 Shew me a penny. Whose image and superscription hath it? 25 Render therefore unto Caesar the things which be Caesar's, and unto God the things which be God's.

To certain of the Sadducees
34 The children of this world marry, and are given in marriage: 35 but they which shall be accounted worthy to obtain that world, and the resurrection from the dead, neither marry, nor are given in marriage: 36 neither can they die any more: for they are equal unto the angels; and are the children of God, being the children of the resurrection. 37 Now that the dead are raised, even Moses shewed at the bush, when he calleth the Lord the God of Abraham, and the God of Isaac, and the God of Jacob. 38 For he is not a God of the dead, but of the living: for all live unto him.

To certain of the scribes
41 How say they that Christ is David's son? 42 And David himself saith in the book of Psalms, The Lord said unto my Lord, Sit thou on my right hand, 43 till I make thine enemies thy footstool. 44 David therefore calleth him Lord, how is he then his son?

To his disciples
46 Beware of the scribes, which desire to walk in long robes, and love greetings in the markets, and the highest seats in the synagogues, and the chief rooms at feasts; 47 which devour widows' houses, and for a shew make long prayers: the same shall receive greater damnation.

Luke 21
By the treasury, to his disciples
3 Of a truth I say unto you, that this poor widow hath cast in more than they all: 4 for all these have of their abundance cast in unto the offerings of God: but she of her penury hath cast in all the living that she had.

Concerning the temple
6 As for these things which ye behold, the days will come, in which there shall not be left one stone upon another, that shall not be thrown down. When asked "What sign will there be when these

things come to pass?" 8 Take heed that ye be not deceived: for many shall come in my name, saying, I am Christ; and the time draweth near: go ye not therefore after them. 9 But when ye shall hear of wars and commotions, be not terrified: for these things must first come to pass; but the end is not by and by.10 Nation shall rise against nation, and kingdom against kingdom: 11 and great earthquakes shall be in divers places, and famines, and pestilences; and fearful sights and great signs shall there be from heaven. 12 But before all these, they shall lay their hands on you, and persecute you, delivering you up to the synagogues, and into prisons, being brought before kings and rulers for my name's sake. 13 And it shall turn to you for a testimony. 14 Settle it therefore in your hearts, not to meditate before what ye shall answer: 15 for I will give you a mouth and wisdom, which all your adversaries shall not be able to gainsay nor resist. 16 And ye shall be betrayed both by parents, and brethren, and kinsfolks, and friends; and some of you shall they cause to be put to death.17 And ye shall be hated of all men for my name's sake. 18 But there shall not an hair of your head perish. 19 In your patience possess ye your souls. 20 And when ye shall see Jerusalem compassed with armies, then know that the desolation thereof is nigh. 21 Then let them which are in Judaea flee to the mountains; and let them which are in the midst of it depart out; and let not them that are in the countries enter thereinto. 22 For these be the days of vengeance, that all things which are written may be fulfilled. 23 But woe unto them that are with child, and to them that give suck, in those days! For there shall be great distress in the land, and wrath upon this people. 24 And they shall fall by the edge of the sword, and shall be led away captive into all nations: and Jerusalem shall be trodden down of the Gentiles, until the times of the Gentiles be fulfilled.25 And there shall be signs in the sun, and in the moon, and in the stars; and upon the earth distress of nations, with perplexity; the sea and the waves roaring; 26 Men's hearts failing them for fear, and for looking after those things which are coming on the earth: for the powers of heaven shall be shaken. 27 And then shall they see the Son of man coming in a cloud with power and great glory. 28 And when these things begin to come to pass, then look up, and lift up your heads; for your redemption draweth nigh.29 And he spake to them a parable; Behold the fig tree, and all the trees; 30 when they now shoot forth, ye see and know of your own selves that summer is now nigh at hand. 31 So likewise ye, when ye see these things come to pass, know ye that the kingdom of God is nigh at hand. 32 Verily I say unto you, this generation shall not pass away, till all be fulfilled. 33 Heaven and earth shall pass away: but my words shall not pass away. 34 And take heed to yourselves, lest at any time your hearts be overcharged with surfeiting, and drunkenness, and cares of this life, and so that day come upon you unawares. 35 For as a snare shall it come on all them that dwell on the face of the whole earth. 36 Watch ye therefore, and pray always, that ye may be accounted worthy to escape all these things that shall come to pass, and to stand before the Son of man.

DEVOTION

Price Tag or Price Paid?

Luke 20:46 is where we want to focus today! Beware of the scribes who walk in long robes, love to sit in the highest seats and in the chief rooms. They like to pray long prayers and be seen.

In Matthew, He says, "These so-called ministers have their reward". Jesus is saying don't be like those who must be stroked and rewarded for showing up! Who must sit with the highest and be seen with the best! Keeping up the image! No! Be like those who pray regardless of who is in the room...5, 500 or 5000. Don't be so good you can't be seen unless it's on the expensive rack with the others! NO! Be like this: be like those who are rich in faith. It's not a bad thing to have riches and be famous for Christ's sake, rather it's quite biblical! He told Abraham, "I will make your name great". However, our focus should not be on our temporary popularity of people but our eternal popularity to God! Does He know our name? Is HE pleased?

Don't equate your value to God with how people value you. Your net worth doesn't determine your God worth! Jesus said to His disciples after they had cast out demons, "Don't rejoice about this, rather rejoice that your name is written in the book of life". Today see yourself valuable to God! Everything that you have gone through is literally been a process to become more powerful. Stay intimate with God! When God is ready to use you, you won't have to pray long prayers. You will already be prepared! You will press into what God has for you without the need to step on someone to get seen! God will make sure you are seen!

What did the words of Jesus speak to you today?

_____

_____

_____

_____

_____

How can you apply them to your life?

_____

_____

_____

_____

_____

Luke 22
To Peter and John
8 Go and prepare us the passover, that we may eat.
10 Behold, when ye are entered into the city, there shall a man meet you, bearing a pitcher of water; follow him into the house where he entereth in. 11 And ye shall say unto the good man of the house, The Master saith unto thee, Where is the guest chamber, where I shall eat the passover with my disciples? 12 And he shall shew you a large upper room furnished: there make ready.

At the Passover, to the twelve apostles
15 With desire I have desired to eat this passover with you before I suffer: 16 for I say unto you, I will not any more eat thereof, until it be fulfilled in the kingdom of God. 17 And he took the cup, and gave thanks, "Take this, and divide it among yourselves: 18 for I say unto you, I will not drink of the fruit of the vine, until the kingdom of God shall come. 19 And he took bread, and gave thanks, and brake it, and gave unto them, This is my body which is given for you: this do in remembrance of me." 20 Likewise also the cup after supper, this cup is the new testament in my blood, which is shed for you. 21 But, behold, the hand of him that betrayeth me is with me on the table. 22 And truly the Son of man goeth, as it was determined: but woe unto that man by whom he is betrayed!

To the apostles
25 The kings of the Gentiles exercise lordship over them; and they that exercise authority upon them are called benefactors. 26 But ye shall not be so: but he that is greatest among you, let him be as the younger; and he that is chief, as he that doth serve. 27 For whether is greater, he that sitteth at meat, or he that serveth? Is not he that sitteth at meat? But I am among you as he that serveth. 28 Ye are they which have continued with me in my temptations. 29 And I appoint unto you a kingdom, as my Father hath appointed unto me; 30 that ye may eat and drink at my table in my kingdom, and sit on thrones judging the twelve tribes of Israel.

To Simon (Peter)
31 Simon, Simon, behold, Satan hath desired to have you, that he may sift you as wheat: 32 but I have prayed for thee, that thy faith fail not: and when thou art converted, strengthen thy brethren. 34 I tell thee, Peter, the cock shall not crow this day, before that thou shalt thrice deny that thou knowest me.

To his disciples
35 When I sent you without purse, and scrip, and shoes, lacked ye anything? 36 But now, he that hath a purse, let him take it, and likewise his scrip: and he that hath no sword, let him sell his garment, and buy one. 37 For I say unto you, that this that is written must yet be accomplished in me, And he was reckoned among the transgressors: for the things concerning me have an end. 38 And they said, Lord, behold, here are two swords. It is enough. At the Mount of Olives, to his disciples 40 Pray that ye enter not into temptation.

Praying to his Father
42 Father, if thou be willing, remove this cup from me: nevertheless not my will, but thine, be done.

To his disciples
46 Why sleep ye? Rise and pray, lest ye enter into temptation.

To Judas
48 Judas, betrayest thou the Son of man with a kiss?

To the one who cut off the ear of the servant of the high priest
51 Suffer ye thus far. And he touched his ear, and healed him.

To the chief priests, captains of the temple,and the elders
52 Be ye come out, as against a thief, with swords and staves? 53 When I was daily with you in the temple, ye stretched forth no hands against me: but this is your hour, and the power of darkness.

At the council, to the elders, the chief priests and the scribes
67 If I tell you, ye will not believe: 68 and if I also ask you, ye will not answer me, nor let me go. 69 Hereafter shall the Son of man sit on the right hand of the power of God. 70 Then said they all, Art thou then the Son of God? Ye say that I am.

Luke 23
When Pilate asks, "Art thou the King of the Jews?"
3 Thou sayest it.

While Simon, a Cyrenian, carried Jesus' cross, to the women that wailed and lamented
28 Daughters of Jerusalem, weep not for me, but weep for yourselves, and for your children. 29 For, behold, the days are coming, in the which they shall say, Blessed are the barren, and the wombs that never bare, and the paps which never gave suck. 30 Then shall they begin to say to the mountains, Fall on us; and to the hills, Cover us. 31 For if they do these things in a green tree, what shall be done in the dry?

On the cross, to his Father
34 Father, forgive them; for they know not what they do.
To one of the malefactors 43 Verily I say unto thee, To-day shalt thou be with me in paradise.

To his Father
46 Father, into thy hands I commend my spirit:

Luke 24
On the road to Emmaus, to two disciples
17 What manner of communications are these that ye have one to another, as ye walk, and are sad? When asked if he does not know of the things which have just come to pass. 19 What things? 25 O fools, and slow of heart to believe all that the prophets have spoken: 26 Ought not Christ to have suffered these things, and to enter into his glory?

In Jerusalem, appearing in the midst of the eleven disciples
36 Peace be unto you. 38 Why are ye troubled? And why do thoughts arise in your hearts? 39 Behold my hands and my feet, that it is I myself: handle me, and see; for a spirit hath not flesh and bones, as ye see me have. 41 Have ye here any meat? 44 These are the words which I spake unto you, while I was yet with you, that all things must be fulfilled, which were written in the law of Moses, and in the prophets, and in the psalms, concerning me.

To the disciples, before he was parted from them, and carried up into heaven
46 Thus it is written, and thus it behoved Christ to suffer, and to rise from the dead the third day: 47 and that repentance and remission of sins should be preached in his name among all nations, beginning at Jerusalem. 48 And ye are witnesses of these things. 49 And, behold, I send the promise of my Father upon you: but tarry ye in the city of Jerusalem, until ye be endued with power from on high.

DEVOTION

Upset or Setup?

Here we are winding up the book of Luke. He's preparing a Passover, He eats with the disciples, He shares with Peter that Satan has desired to take him, He prays for His father to remove the cup which is the crucifixion and the season He must walk through, He is brought before the chief priests and the elders and is gorged, yet as He is hung up on the cross His words were, "Father forgive them for they don't know what they're doing".

Can you do that? Can you let your pride down and your emotional attachment to those who are spitefully using you and speaking negative about you? Even your closest friends are about to deny you and people are spitting on you, pulling your beard, tripping you on the way through life and talking about you behind your back. Can you say father forgive them? Everyone wants to be like Jesus up until this moment! Everyone wants resurrection in their life but in order to have resurrection you've got to have some crucifixion. Haters are not your motivators, they are your prayer assignments! The true authenticity of Christianity is forgiveness, repentance and walking in the kingdom. Sure it's hard! Absolutely you're going to feel shafted, put down, beat up and thrown away at times. Yes life is going to make you feel like you're disposable and there's no need for you. But your UPSETS ARE SETUPS!

Today don't let any setbacks hold you back! Know that the Bible says in Romans 8 that all things work together for the good! Everything that happens to you God can make bloom! After all, fertile soil is not on the mountain tops, it is always in the valley for that is where all of the nutrients are found to grow incredible fruit. Stuff that is grown in the mountains are things like coffee...stimulants! What God is putting in you through your upsets is His character, integrity, fruit on the vine, and the ability to sustain yourself in the mountain experience.

What did the words of Jesus speak to you today?

_____

_____

_____

_____

_____

How can you apply them to your life?

_____

_____

_____

_____

_____

The Gospel According to John

John 1
33 Upon whom thou shalt see the Spirit descending, and remaining on him, the same is he which baptizeth with the Holy Spirit.

Holy Ghost.
38 What seek ye? 39 Come and see.

To Simon
42 Thou art Simon the son of Jona: thou shalt be called Cephas

In Galilee, to Philip
43 Follow me.

To Nathanael
47 Behold an Israelite indeed, in whom is no guile! 48 Before that Philip called thee, when thou wast under the fig tree, I saw thee. 50 Because I said unto thee, I saw thee under the fig tree, believest thou? Thou shalt see greater things than these. 51 Verily, verily, I say unto you, Hereafter ye shall see heaven open, and the angels of God ascending and descending upon the Son of man.

At the marriage feast in Cana of Galilee, to his mother
John 2
4 Woman, what have I to do with thee? Mine hour is not yet come.

To the servants
7 Fill the water pots with water. 8 Draw out now, and bear unto the governor of the feast.

At the temple in Jerusalem, to them that sold doves
16 Take these things hence; make not my Father's house an house of merchandise.

To the Jews
19 Destroy this temple, and in three days I will raise it up.

John 3
To Nicodemus
3 Verily, verily, I say unto thee, Except a man be born again, he cannot see the kingdom of God. 5 Verily, verily, I say unto thee, Except a man be born of water and of the Spirit, he cannot enter into the kingdom of God. 6 that which is born of the flesh is flesh; and that which is born of the Spirit is spirit. 7 Marvel not that I said unto thee, Ye must be born again. 8 The wind bloweth where it listeth, and thou hearest the sound thereof, but canst not tell whence it cometh, and whither it goeth: so is every one that is born of the Spirit. 10 Art thou a master of Israel, and knowest not these things?
11 Verily, verily, I say unto thee, We speak that we do know, and testify that we have seen; and ye receive not our witness. 12 If I have told you earthly things, and ye believe not, how shall ye believe, if I tell you of heavenly things? 13 And no man hath ascended up to heaven, but he that came down from heaven, even the Son of man which is in heaven. 14 And as Moses lifted up the serpent in the wilderness, even so must the Son of man be lifted up: 15 that whosoever believeth in him should not perish, but have eternal life. 16 For God so loved the world, that he gave his only

begotten Son, that whosoever believeth in him should not perish, but have everlasting life. 17 For God sent not his Son into the world to condemn the world; but that the world through him might be saved. 18 He that believeth on him is not condemned: but he that believeth not is condemned already, because he hath not believed in the name of the only begotten Son of God. 19 And this is the condemnation, that light is come into the world, and men loved darkness rather than light, because their deeds were evil. 20 For every one that doeth evil hateth the light, neither cometh to the light, lest his deeds should be reproved. 21 But he that doeth truth cometh to the light, that his deeds may be made manifest, that they are wrought in God.

John 4
At Jacob's well, to a woman of Samaria
7 Give me to drink. 10 If thou knewest the gift of God, and who it is that saith to thee, Give me to drink; thou wouldest have asked of him, and he would have given thee living water. 13 Whosoever drinketh of this water shall thirst again: 14 but whosoever drinketh of the water that I shall give him shall never thirst; but the water that I shall give him shall be in him a well of water springing up into everlasting life. 16 Go, call thy husband, and come hither. 17 Thou hast well said, I have no husband: 18 for thou hast had five husbands; and he whom thou now hast is not thy husband: in that saidst thou truly. 21 Woman, believe me, the hour cometh, when ye shall neither in this mountain, nor yet at Jerusalem, worship the Father. 22 Ye worship ye know not what: we know what we worship: for salvation is of the Jews. 23 But the hour cometh, and now is, when the true worshippers shall worship the Father in spirit and in truth: for the Father seeketh such to worship him. 24 God is a Spirit: and they that worship him must worship him in spirit and in truth. 26 I that speak unto thee am he.

To his disciples
32 I have meat to eat that ye know not of. 34 My meat is to do the will of him that sent me, and to finish his work. 35 Say not ye, There are yet four months, and then cometh harvest? Behold, I say unto you, Lift up your eyes, and look on the fields; for they are white already to harvest. 36 And he that reapeth receiveth wages, and gathereth fruit unto life eternal: that both he that soweth and he that reapeth may rejoice together. 37 And herein is that saying true, One soweth, and another reapeth. 38 I sent you to reap that whereon ye bestowed no labour: other men laboured, and ye are entered into their labours. In Cana of Galilee, to a nobleman whose son was sick 48 Except ye see signs and wonders, ye will not believe. 50 Go thy way; thy son liveth.

DEVOTION

Can God Use Your Dirty Vessel?

What I love about the story in John 2 is not mentioned in the words of Jesus. The Bible says that when they said they ran out of wine His mother says, "Do something here". Jesus says, "My time has not yet come". She, still being persistent says to the servants, "Do whatever Jesus tells you to do and don't question it".

Jesus told them to go over by the front door and fill those vessels up and bring some to the master of the feast! Don't miss what the Scriptures say in this...it's phenomenal. It says those vessels were according to the manner of purification. In other words, those vessels were the water pots that everybody washed their hands and feet in. HELLO? Anybody seeing this? Wow! Jesus is telling them go get the dirty water pots! Fill them up!

Here's the catch...somewhere from filling them up, drawing them out and walking them to the master, the water changed to wine! It is not our responsibility to change the water to wine! Our responsibility is to fill them up, draw them out, and walk them to the master. Nowhere in this passage does Jesus say to make sure the water is clean and make sure that it turns to wine before the master gets it. It simply says the servants were to do what Jesus said to do.

This means God can use anybody! He can use the dirtiest of the dirty! He can use those who everyone else has washed their hands of and stepped on! That's right...you're not too awful or have done something so terrible that Jesus could not use you. Jesus can use what He wants to use to bring His glory. Today, get yourself filled up. Today, get yourself moving towards the master. Today is your day to turn your water to wine! At the end of the story the master says, "You have saved the best for last". This means that even though you started out good or you started out bad...it makes no difference. Surrender to a faith-filled life and watch God make your greatest season come.

What did the words of Jesus speak to you today?

_____
_____
_____
_____
_____

How can you apply them to your life?

_____
_____
_____
_____
_____

John 5
At the pool called Bethesda, to a man which had an infirmity
6 Wilt thou be made whole? 8 Rise, take up thy bed, and walk.

In the temple, to the healed man
14 Behold, thou art made whole: sin no more, lest a worse thing come unto thee.

To the Jews
17 My Father worketh hitherto, and I work. 19 Verily, verily, I say unto you, The Son can do nothing of himself, but what he seeth the Father do: for what things so ever he doeth, these also doeth the Son likewise. 20 For the Father loveth the Son, and sheweth him all things that himself doeth: and he will shew him greater works than these, that ye may marvel. 21 For as the Father raiseth up the dead, and quickeneth them; even so the Son quickeneth whom he will.
22 For the Father judgeth no man, but hath committed all judgment unto the Son: 23 that all men should honour the Son, even as they honour the Father. He that honoureth not the Son honoureth not the Father which hath sent him. 24 Verily, verily, I say unto you, He that heareth my word, and believeth on him that sent me, hath everlasting life, and shall not come into condemnation; but is passed from death unto life. 25 Verily, verily, I say unto you, The hour is coming, and now is, when the dead shall hear the voice of the Son of God: and they that hear shall live. 26 For as the Father hath life in himself; so hath he given to the Son to have life in himself; 27 and hath given him authority to execute judgment also, because he is the Son of man. 28 Marvel not at this: for the hour is coming, in the which all that are in the graves shall hear his voice, 29 and shall come forth; they that have done good, unto the resurrection of life; and they that have done evil, unto the resurrection of damnation. 30 I can of mine own self do nothing: as I hear, I judge: and my judgment is just; because I seek not mine own will, but the will of the Father which hath sent me. 31 If I bear witness of myself, my witness is not true. 32 There is another that beareth witness of me; and I know that the witness which he witnesseth of me is true. 33 Ye sent unto John, and he bare witness unto the truth. 34 But I receive not testimony from man: but these things I say, that ye might be saved. 35 He was a burning and a shining light: and ye were willing for a season to rejoice in his light. 36 But I have greater witness than that of John: for the works which the Father hath given me to finish, the same works that I do, bear witness of me, that the Father hath sent me. 37 And the Father himself, which hath sent me, hath borne witness of me. Ye have neither heard his voice at any time, nor seen his shape. 38 And ye have not his word abiding in you: for whom he hath sent, him ye believe not. 39 Search the scriptures; for in them ye think ye have eternal life: and they are they which testify of me. 40 And ye will not come to me, that ye might have life. 41 I receive not honour from men. 42 But I know you, that ye have not the love of God in you. 43 I am come in my Father's name, and ye receive me not: if another shall come in his own name, him ye will receive. 44 How can ye believe, which receive honour one of another, and seek not the honour that cometh from God only? 45 Do not think that I will accuse you to the Father: there is one that accuseth you, even Moses, in whom ye trust. 46 For had ye believed Moses, ye would have believed me: for he wrote of me. 47 But if ye believe not his writings, how shall ye believe my words?

John 6
On a mountain, to Philip, concerning the multitude
5 Whence shall we buy bread, that these may eat?

To his disciples
10 Make the men sit down. 12 Gather up the fragments that remain, that nothing be lost.

On the sea, to his disciples
20 It is I; be not afraid.

At Capernaum, in the temple, to the people
26 Verily, verily, I say unto you, Ye seek me, not because ye saw the miracles, but because ye did eat of the loaves, and were filled. 27 Labour not for the meat which perisheth, but for that meat which endureth unto everlasting life, which the Son of man shall give unto you: for him hath God the Father sealed. 29 This is the work of God that ye believe on him whom he hath sent. 32 Verily, verily, I say unto you, Moses gave you not that bread from heaven; but my Father giveth you the true bread from heaven. 33 For the bread of God is he which cometh down from heaven, and giveth life unto the world. 35 I am the bread of life: he that cometh to me shall never hunger; and he that believeth on me shall never thirst. 36 But I said unto you, That ye also have seen me, and believe not. 37 All that the Father giveth me shall come to me; and him that cometh to me I will in no wise cast out. 38 For I came down from heaven, not to do mine own will, but the will of him that sent me. 39 And this is the Father's will which hath sent me, that of all which he hath given me I should lose nothing, but should raise it up again at the last day. 40 And this is the will of him that sent me, that every one which seeth the Son, and believeth on him, may have everlasting life: and I will raise him up at the last day.

DEVOTION

The Judgment Seat of Christ

Verse 22 says that Jesus has been given the responsibility to judge. Wow! The good thing about that is He has walked in our shoes and knows the struggle.

There is a very popular saying right now that says, "Only God can judge me". The reason people wear the shirt and tattoo themselves with this saying is because they are tired of people judging them for what they have done, or more aggressively, what they continue to do regardless if the Bible says not to. The truth is that they are right! ONLY GOD CAN JUDGE THEM...but what they fail to remember is that one day HE WILL!! He will judge all of us.

Grace was never for us to continue in our sin. John 5:14 makes it very clear that after He healed the man in the temple He said these words, "Sin no more, lest a worse thing come unto thee". This gives us revelation that some types of issues we are struggling with come from the fact that we have sinned and opened a door for ourselves to be out from under the protection of walking in covenant with God.

Jesus has a judgement seat as well as a mercy seat. Sometimes when we focus only on the grace and mercy, we give ourselves a hall pass to do whatever we think is okay and it's not. We open up ourselves for destruction. Things down on earth happen. No, Jesus is not punishing us all the time. No, God is not waiting for the moment for you to mess up so He can disqualify you. However, we disqualify ourselves when we walk away from the covenant protections and provisions. Jesus tells the Jews, you keep avoiding Me, not believing in Me and one day I will not be so merciful to those who continue to reject Me. Thank God for mercy and thank God for grace, but keep the fear of God in your heart. (Not being afraid, but keeping Him first and reverencing Him!)

What did the words of Jesus speak to you today?

_____

_____

_____

_____

_____

How can you apply them to your life?

_____

_____

_____

_____

_____

John 6
To the Jews

43 Murmur not among yourselves. 44 No man can come to me, except the Father which hath sent me draw him: and I will raise him up at the last day. 45 It is written in the prophets, And they shall be all taught of God. Every man therefore that hath heard, and hath learned of the Father, cometh unto me. 46 Not that any man hath seen the Father, save he which is of God, he hath seen the Father. 47 Verily, verily, I say unto you, He that believeth on me hath everlasting life. 48 I am that bread of life. 49 Your fathers did eat manna in the wilderness, and are dead. 50 This is the bread which cometh down from heaven, that a man may eat thereof, and not die. 51 I am the living bread which came down from heaven: if any man eat of this bread, he shall live forever: and the bread that I will give is my flesh, which I will give for the life of the world. 53 Verily, verily, I say unto you, Except ye eat the flesh of the Son of man, and drink his blood, ye have no life in you. 54 Whoso eateth my flesh, and drinketh my blood, hath eternal life; and I will raise him up at the last day. 55 For my flesh is meat indeed, and my blood is drink indeed. 56 He that eateth my flesh, and drinketh my blood, dwelleth in me, and I in him. 57 As the living Father hath sent me, and I live by the Father: so he that eateth me, even he shall live by me. 58 This is that bread which came down from heaven: not as your fathers did eat manna, and are dead: he that eateth of this bread shall live for ever.

To his disciples

61 Doth this offend you? 62 What and if ye shall see the Son of man ascend up where he was before? 63 It is the spirit that quickeneth; the flesh profiteth nothing: the words that I speak unto you, they are spirit, and they are life. 64 But there are some of you that believe not. 65 Therefore said I unto you, that no man can come unto me, except it were given unto him of my Father.

Unto the twelve

67 Will ye also go away? 70 Have not I chosen you twelve, and one of you is a devil?

John 7
In Galilee, to his brethren

6 My time is not yet come: but your time is alway ready. 7 The world cannot hate you; but me it hateth, because I testify of it, that the works thereof are evil. 8 Go ye up unto this feast: I go not up yet unto this feast; for my time is not yet full come.

At the temple in Jerusalem, to the Jews

16 My doctrine is not mine, but his that sent me. 17 If any man will do his will, he shall know of the doctrine, whether it be of God, or whether I speak of myself. 18 He that speaketh of himself seeketh his own glory: but he that seeketh his glory that sent him, the same is true, and no unrighteousness is in him. 19 Did not Moses give you the law, and yet none of you keepeth the law? Why go ye about to kill me? 21 I have done one work, and ye all marvel. 22 Moses therefore gave unto you circumcision; (not because it is of Moses, but of the fathers;) and ye on the Sabbath day circumcise a man. 23 If a man on the Sabbath day receive circumcision, that the law of Moses should not be broken; are ye angry at me, because I have made a man every whit whole on the Sabbath day? 24 Judge not according to the appearance, but judge righteous judgment. 28 Ye both know me, and ye know whence I am: and I am not come of myself, but he that sent me is true, whom ye know not. 29 But I know him: for I am from him, and he hath sent me.

To the officers of the Pharisees and the chief priests

33 Yet a little while am I with you, and then I go unto him that sent me. 34 Ye shall seek me, and shall not find me: and where I am, thither ye cannot come.

To the Jews
37 If any man thirsts, let him come unto me, and drink.
38 He that believeth on me, as the scripture hath said, out of his belly shall flow rivers of living water.

Chapter 8
In Jerusalem, in the temple, to the scribes and Pharisees, concerning the woman taken in adultery
7 He that is without sin among you, let him first cast a stone at her.

To the adulterous woman
10 Woman, where are those thine accusers? Hath no man condemned thee? 11 Neither do I condemn thee: go, and sin no more.

In the treasury of the temple, to the scribes and Pharisees,
12 I am the light of the world: he that followeth me shall not walk in darkness, but shall have the light of life. 14 Though I bear record of myself, yet my record is true: for I know whence I came, and whither I go; but ye cannot tell whence I come, and whither I go. 15 Ye judge after the flesh; I judge no man. 16 And yet if I judge, my judgment is true: for I am not alone, but I and the Father that sent me. 17 It is also written in your law, that the testimony of two men is true. 18 I am one that bear witness of myself, and the Father that sent me beareth witness of me. 19 Ye neither know me, nor my Father: if ye had known me, ye should have known my Father also. 21 I go my way, and ye shall seek me, and shall die in your sins: whither I go, ye cannot come.

To the Jews
23 Ye are from beneath; I am from above: ye are of this world; I am not of this world. 24 I said therefore unto you, that ye shall die in your sins: for if ye believe not that I am he, ye shall die in your sins. 25 Even the same that I said unto you from the beginning. 26 I have many things to say and to judge of you: but he that sent me is true; and I speak to the world those things which I have heard of him. 28 When ye have lifted up the Son of man, then shall ye know that I am he, and that I do nothing of myself; but as my Father hath taught me, I speak these things. 29 And he that sent me is with me: the Father hath not left me alone; for I do always those things that please him.

DEVOTION

A License to Kill

There is so much in this day that is great to do a devotion on but let's focus on John 10:7 where the woman has been caught in the very act of adultery.

Can you imagine the shame this woman felt as it was not told that she had done something, she was doing it as they walked in? This woman was a sinner and just got done having sex with a man who was married. That's horrible! She is partly to blame for a marriage and family that will be busted up possibly from her lust and actions

They drug her to the feet of Jesus and said to Him, "The law of Moses demands this woman be stoned". Jesus replied by saying, "He that is without sin, let him cast a stone". After He made a public spectacle of their judgmental attitude, He alone is left with this sinner woman. Jesus had just said he that is without sin should cast the stones. Here Jesus is our high priest who knows no sin. He is without sin! Out of His own mouth He declared He is the one that has the license to kill this woman! But He never picks up a stone! This shows us what we should be like if we are like Jesus. He had the power to throw the stone but He didn't! Wow! Can we do that?!

He tells her to go and SIN NO MORE! Again, we see Him saying don't do that again because it's going to open up some things to you again!

The two evil twins of grace and mercy are shame and guilt. Jesus gives us grace for our guilt and mercy for our shame. Let's do the same for others when they don't add up to our qualifications of being a Christian!

What did the words of Jesus speak to you today?

_____
_____
_____
_____
_____

How can you apply them to your life?

_____
_____
_____
_____
_____

To the Jews which believed on him

31 If ye continue in my word, then are ye my disciples indeed; 32 and ye shall know the truth, and the truth shall make you free. 34 Verily, verily, I say unto you, whosoever committeth sin is the servant of sin. 35 And the servant abideth not in the house for ever: but the Son abideth ever. 36 If the Son therefore shall make you free, ye shall be free indeed. 37 I know that ye are Abraham's seed; but ye seek to kill me, because my word hath no place in you. 38 I speak that which I have seen with my Father: and ye do that which ye have seen with your father. 39 If ye were Abraham's children, ye would do the works of Abraham. 40 But now ye seek to kill me, a man that hath told you the truth, which I have heard of God: this did not Abraham. 41 Ye do the deeds of your father. 42 If God were your Father, ye would love me: for I proceeded forth and came from God; neither came I of myself, but he sent me. 43 Why do ye not understand my speech? Even because ye cannot hear my word. 44 Ye are of your father the devil, and the lusts of your father ye will do. He was a murderer from the beginning, and abode not in the truth, because there is no truth in him. When he speaketh a lie, he speaketh of his own: for he is a liar, and the father of it. 45 And because I tell you the truth, ye believe me not. 46 Which of you convinceth me of sin? And if I say the truth, why do ye not believe me? 47 He that is of God heareth God's words: ye therefore hear them not, because ye are not of God. 49 I have not a devil; but I honour my Father, and ye do dishonour me. 50 And I seek not mine own glory: there is one that seeketh and judgeth. 51 Verily, verily, I say unto you, If a man keep my saying, he shall never see death. 54 If I honour myself, my honour is nothing: it is my Father that honoureth me; of whom ye say, that he is your God: 55 yet ye have not known him; but I know him: and if I should say, I know him not, I shall be a liar like unto you: but I know him, and keep his saying. 56 Your father Abraham rejoiced to see my day: and he saw it, and was glad. 58 Verily, verily, I say unto you, Before Abraham was, I am.

John 9
To his disciples, concerning a blind man

3 Neither hath this man sinned, nor his parents: but that the works of God should be made manifest in him. 4 I must work the works of him that sent me, while it is day: the night cometh, when no man can work. 5 As long as I am in the world, I am the light of the world.

To the blind man

7 Go, wash in the pool of Siloam, 35 Dost thou believe on the Son of God? 37 Thou hast both seen him, and it is he that talketh with thee. 39 For judgment I am come into this world, that they which see not might see; and that they which see might be made blind.

To the Pharisees

41 If ye were blind, ye should have no sin: but now ye say, We see; therefore your sin remaineth.

John 10

1 Verily, verily, I say unto you, He that entereth not by the door into the sheepfold, but climbeth up some other way, the same is a thief and a robber. 2 But he that entereth in by the door is the shepherd of the sheep. 3 To him the porter openeth; and the sheep hear his voice: and he calleth his own sheep by name, and leadeth them out. 4 And when he putteth forth his own sheep, he goeth before them, and the sheep follow him: for they know his voice. 5 And a stranger will they not follow, but will flee from him: for they know not the voice of strangers. 7 Verily, verily, I say unto you, I am the door of the sheep. 8 All that ever came before me are thieves and robbers: but the sheep did not hear them.
9 I am the door: by me if any man enter in, he shall be saved, and shall go in and out, and find pasture. 10 The thief cometh not, but for to steal, and to kill, and to destroy: I am come that they

might have life, and that they might have it more abundantly. 11 I am the good shepherd: the good shepherd giveth his life for the sheep. 12 But he that is an hireling, and not the shepherd, whose own the sheep are not, seeth the wolf coming, and leaveth the sheep, and fleeth: and the wolf catcheth them, and scattereth the sheep. 13 The hireling fleeth, because he is an hireling, and careth not for the sheep. 14 I am the good shepherd, and know my sheep, and am known of mine. 15 As the Father knoweth me, even so know I the Father: and I lay down my life for the sheep. 16 And other sheep I have, which are not of this fold: them also I must bring, and they shall hear my voice; and there shall be one fold, and one shepherd. 17 Therefore doth my Father love me, because I lay down my life, that I might take it again. 18 No man taketh it from me, but I lay it down of myself. I have power to lay it down, and I have power to take it again. This commandment have I received of my Father.

In the temple onSolomon's porch, to the Jews
25 I told you, and ye believed not: the works that I do in my Father's name, they bear witness of me. 26 But ye believe not, because ye are not of my sheep, as I said unto you. 27 My sheep hear my voice, and I know them, and they follow me: 28 and I give unto them eternal life; and they shall never perish, neither shall any man pluck them out of my hand. 29 My Father, which gave them me, is greater than all; and no man is able to pluck them out of my Father's hand. 30 I and my Father are one. 32 Many good works have I shewed you from my Father; for which of those works do ye stone me? 34 Is it not written in your law, I said, Ye are gods? 35 If he called them gods, unto whom the word of God came, and the scripture cannot be broken; 36 say ye of him, whom the Father hath sanctified, and sent into the world, Thou blasphemest; because I said, I am the Son of God? 37 If I do not the works of my Father, believe me not. 38 But if I do, though ye believe not me, believe the works: that ye may know, and believe, that the Father is in me, and I in him.

DEVOTION

Who's the Thief???

John 10 gives us great insight on what a true shepherd is. It starts off by talking about people who are shepherding sheep. Obviously this is talking about people in leadership concerning God's people. Jesus goes on to say that He is the good shepherd and a good shepherd gives his life for the sheep. However, a hireling is a shepherd who leaves when they see the wolf coming.

Often people say, "The devil comes to steal, kill and destroy". This is quoted from John 10:10. Yes, the devil does steal, kill and destroy, but in the context of this message, Jesus is pointing out hirelings to be people who are shepherds but really don't care about the sheep! They're in it for themselves, shearing the sheep and enjoying the benefits and blessings of this shepherding business. If the thief was the devil, then who is the wolf? The thief then has to be false shepherds, who when the wolf (devil) comes, they leave and run!

Many people say that when Jesus was younger and said the words, "I am about my father's business", that the word business is what we need to look at church as...doing business. Listen! This is not against church business but here's how it should go: we should be a church that has a business in it, we should never be a business that runs a church. Churches who put business first hurt people, don't care about people, only care about numbers, not in it to take people to green pastures, but in it to make green-filled wallets. They falsely look like shepherds.

How can you tell the difference? You can't until the wolf comes!! The point is that when you are going through an attack and the shepherd sees it and runs, you may be in the wrong church.

However, if your Pastors/church staff don't see it because you haven't notified them, it's not something they can help. God wants us to put Him first! He is the true shepherd! Jesus cries out however, and says later on, "God, give these people shepherds". Do we ever need true shepherds that will flank the side of the believers in times of trial! That don't run when the fire gets hot!

What did the words of Jesus speak to you today?

_____
_____
_____
_____
_____

How can you apply them to your life?

_____
_____
_____
_____
_____

John 11
Concerning Lazarus
4 This sickness is not unto death, but for the glory of God, that the Son of God might be glorified thereby.

To his disciples
7 Let us go into Judaea again. 9 Are there not twelve hours in the day? If any man walk in the day, he stumbleth not, because he seeth the light of this world. 10 But if a man walk in the night, he stumbleth, because there is no light in him. 11Our friend Lazarus sleepeth; but I go, that I may awake him out of sleep. 14 Lazarus is dead. 15 And I am glad for your sakes that I was not there, to the intent ye may believe; nevertheless let us go unto him.

In Bethany, to Martha
23 Thy brother shall rise again. 25 I am the resurrection, and the life: he that believeth in me, though he were dead, yet shall he live: 26 and whosoever liveth and believeth in me shall never die. Believest thou this?

To Mary and the Jews
34 Where have ye laid him?

At the cave where Lazarus was laid
39 Take ye away the stone.

To Martha
40 Said I not unto thee, that, if thou wouldest believe, thou shouldest see the glory of God?

Speaking to his Father
41 Father, I thank thee that thou hast heard me. 42 And I knew that thou hearest me always: but because of the people which stand by I said it, that they may believe that thou hast sent me.

To Lazarus
43 Lazarus, come forth. And he that was dead came forth,

To the Jews
44 Loose him, and let him go.

John 12
At Bethany, six days before the Passover, to Judas Iscariot
7 Let her alone: against the day of my burying hath she kept this. 8 For the poor always ye have with you; but me ye have not always.

To Andrew and Philip
23 The hour is come, that the Son of man should be glorified. 24 Verily, verily, I say unto you, Except a corn of wheat fall into the ground and die, it abideth alone: but if it die, it bringeth forth much fruit. 25 He that loveth his life shall lose it; and he that hateth his life in this world shall keep it unto life eternal. 26 If any man serve me, let him follow me; and where I am, there shall also my servant be: if any man serve me, him will my Father honour. 27 Now is my soul troubled; and what shall I say? Father, save me from this hour: but for this cause came I unto this hour. 28 Father, glorify thy name. Then came there a voice from heaven, saying, I have both glorified it, and will glorify it again.

To the people

30 This voice came not because of me, but for your sakes.
31 Now is the judgment of this world: now shall the prince of this world be cast out. 32 And I, if I be lifted up from the earth, will draw all men unto me. 35 Yet a little while is the light with you. Walk while ye have the light, lest darkness come upon you: for he that walketh in darkness knoweth not whither he goeth. 36 While ye have light, believe in the light, that ye may be the children of light. 44 He that believeth on me, believeth not on me, but on him that sent me. 45 And he that seeth me seeth him that sent me.
46 I am come a light into the world, that whosoever believeth on me should not abide in darkness. 47 And if any man hear my words, and believe not, I judge him not: for I came not to judge the world, but to save the world. 48 He that rejecteth me, and receiveth not my words, hath one that judgeth him: the word that I have spoken, the same shall judge him in the last day. 49 For I have not spoken of myself; but the Father which sent me, he gave me a commandment, what I should say, and what I should speak. 50 And I know that his commandment is life everlasting: whatsoever I speak therefore, even as the Father said unto me, so I speak.

John 13
After the Passover supper, while washing the disciples' feet, to Peter

7 What I do thou knowest not now; but thou shalt know hereafter. 8 If I wash thee not, thou hast no part with me. 10 He that is washed needeth not save to wash his feet, but is clean every whit: and ye are clean, but not all.

To his disciples

12 Know ye what I have done to you? 13 Ye call me Master and Lord: and ye say well; for so I am. 14 If I then, your Lord and Master, have washed your feet; ye also ought to wash one another's feet. 15 For I have given you an example that ye should do as I have done to you. 16 Verily, verily, I say unto you, The servant is not greater than his lord; neither he that is sent greater than he that sent him. 17 If ye know these things, happy are ye if ye do them. 18 I speak not of you all: I know whom I have chosen: but that the scripture may be fulfilled, He that eateth bread with me hath lifted up his heel against me. 19 Now I tell you before it come, that, when it is come to pass, ye may believe that I am he. 20 Verily, verily, I say unto you, He that receiveth whomsoever I send receiveth me; and he that receiveth me receiveth him that sent me. 21 Verily, verily, I say unto you, that one of you shall betray me. 26 He it is, to whom I shall give a sop, when I have dipped it.

To Judas Iscariot

27 That thou doest, do quickly.

To the eleven disciples

31 Now is the Son of man glorified, and God is glorified in him. 32 If God be glorified in him, God shall also glorify him in himself, and shall straightway glorify him. 33 Little children, yet a little while I am with you. Ye shall seek me: and as I said unto the Jews, Whither I go, ye cannot come; so now I say to you. 34 A new commandment I give unto you, That ye love one another; as I have loved you, that ye also love one another. 35 By this shall all men know that ye are my disciples, if ye have love one to another.

To Simon Peter

36 Whither I go, thou canst not follow me now; but thou shalt follow me afterwards. 38 Wilt thou lay down thy life for my sake? Verily, verily, I say unto thee, The cock shall not crow, till thou hast denied me thrice.

DEVOTION

The G.O.A.T.

Foot washing was a custom in this area of the world. People would take long journeys on foot and then would walk into somebody's house. Basins of water were set beside the front door for them to wash their feet before they entered into a person's house. Also before a communal meal, because tables were lower and feet were in sight, they had to be washed. It was of the lowliest of servants to do the foot washing. Jesus begins to wash the feet of the disciples immediately after they just got done talking about who's going to be the greatest! Jesus shows them who will be the greatest. He also has said the greatest among us is the servant of all. Who wants to be great? A lot of people say they want to be great. They go off and try to be the top of their class, the best in the business, have the largest churches, have the biggest houses and drive the biggest and most expensive cars. But Jesus gives us another view of who is the greatest in this world. He says the greatest among us is a servant of all. If you want to be great in the kingdom of God, have you picked up your towel and found your place of foot washing? No, you may not wash the feet of people, but have you found your place of serving. As pastors, we see hundreds of people, if not thousands, that come to church on Sunday to get empowered, inspired and then leave. We are glad that they are there but many of them have found no place of serving. Servitude is one of the greatest forms of leadership. You cannot be a true leader if you have not found a place of serving. Great leaders were at some time in their lives great followers who knew how to achieve in service to others! That's it! That's the ticket to being the G.O.A.T. - Greatest Of All Time! SERVE...give your life away to people! Love like Jesus and give like Jesus!

What did the words of Jesus speak to you today?

_____

_____

_____

_____

_____

How can you apply them to your life?

_____

_____

_____

_____

_____

John 14
To his disciples

1 Let not your heart be troubled: ye believe in God, believe also in me. 2 In my Father's house are many mansions: if it were not so, I would have told you. I go to prepare a place for you. 3 And if I go and prepare a place for you, I will come again, and receive you unto myself; that where I am, there ye may be also. 4 And whither I go ye know, and the way ye know.

To Thomas

6 I am the way, the truth, and the life: no man cometh unto the Father, but by me. 7 If ye had known me, ye should have known my Father also: and from henceforth ye know him, and have seen him.

To Philip

9 Have I been so long time with you, and yet hast thou not known me, Philip? he that hath seen me hath seen the Father; and how sayest thou then, Shew us the Father? 10 Believest thou not that I am in the Father, and the Father in me? The words that I speak unto you I speak not of myself: but the Father that dwelleth in me, he doeth the works. 11 Believe me that I am in the Father, and the Father in me: or else believe me for the very works' sake. 12 Verily, verily, I say unto you, He that believeth on me, the works that I do shall he do also; and greater works than these shall he do; because I go unto my Father. 13 And whatsoever ye shall ask in my name, that will I do, that the Father may be glorified in the Son. 14 If ye shall ask any thing in my name, I will do it. 15 If ye love me, keep my commandments. 16 And I will pray the Father, and he shall give you another Comforter, that he may abide with you forever; 17 even the Spirit of truth; whom the world cannot receive, because it seeth him not, neither knoweth him: but ye know him; for he dwelleth with you, and shall be in you. 18 I will not leave you comfortless: I will come to you. 19 Yet a little while, and the world seeth me no more; but ye see me: because I live, ye shall live also. 20 At that day ye shall know that I am in my Father, and ye in me, and I in you. 21 He that hath my commandments, and keepeth them, he it is that loveth me: and he that loveth me shall be loved of my Father, and I will love him, and will manifest myself to him.

To Judas (not Iscariot)

23 If a man loves me, he will keep my words: and my Father will love him, and we will come unto him, and make our abode with him. 24 He that loveth me not, keepeth not my sayings: and the word which ye hear is not mine, but the Father's which sent me. 25 These things have I spoken unto you, being yet present with you. 26 But the Comforter, which is the Holy Ghost, whom the Father will send in my name, he shall teach you all things, and bring all things to your remembrance, whatsoever I have said unto you. 27 Peace I leave with you, my peace I give unto you: not as the world giveth, give I unto you. Let not your heart be troubled, neither let it be afraid. 28 Ye have heard how I said unto you, I go away, and come again unto you. If ye loved me, ye would rejoice, because I said, I go unto the Father: for my Father is greater than I. 29 and now I have told you before it come to pass, that, when it is come to pass, ye might believe. 30 Hereafter I will not talk much with you: for the prince of this world cometh, and hath nothing in me. 31 But that the world may know that I love the Father; and as the Father gave me commandment, even so I do. Arise, let us go hence.

John 15

1 I am the true vine, and my Father is the husbandman. 2 Every branch in me that beareth not fruit he taketh away: and every branch that beareth fruit, he purgeth it, that it may bring forth more fruit. 3 Now ye are clean through the word which I have spoken unto you. 4 Abide in me, and I in you. As the branch cannot bear fruit of itself, except it abide in the vine; no more can ye, except ye abide in me. 5 I am the vine, ye are the branches: He that abideth in me, and I in him, the same bringeth forth much fruit: for without me ye can do nothing. 6 If a man abides not in me, he is cast forth as a branch, and is withered; and men gather them, and cast them into the fire, and they are burned. 7 If ye abide in me, and my words abide in you, ye shall ask what ye will, and it shall be done unto you. 8 Herein is my Father glorified, that ye bear much fruit; so shall ye be my disciples. 9 As the Father hath loved me, so have I loved you: continue ye in my love. 10 If ye keep my commandments, ye shall abide in my love; even as I have kept my Father's commandments, and abide in his love. These things have I spoken unto you, that my joy might remain in you, and that your joy might be full. 12 This is my commandment, that ye love one another, as I have loved you. 13 Greater love hath no man than this, that a man lay down his life for his friends. 14 Ye are my friends, if ye do whatsoever I command you. 15 Henceforth I call you not servants; for the servant knoweth not what his lord doeth: but I have called you friends; for all things that I have heard of my Father I have made known unto you. 16 Ye have not chosen me, but I have chosen you, and ordained you, that ye should go and bring forth fruit, and that your fruit should remain: that whatsoever ye shall ask of the Father in my name, he may give it you. 17 These things I command you, that ye love one another. 18 If the world hate you, ye know that it hated me before it hated you. 19 If ye were of the world, the world would love his own: but because ye are not of the world, but I have chosen you out of the world, therefore the world hateth you. 20 Remember the word that I said unto you, The servant is not greater than his lord. If they have persecuted me, they will also persecute you; if they have kept my saying, they will keep yours also. 21 But all these things will they do unto you for my name's sake, because they know not him that sent me. 22 If I had not come and spoken unto them, they had not had sin: but now they have no cloke for their sin. 23 He that hateth me hateth my Father also. 24 If I had not done among them the works which none other man did, they had not had sin: but now have they both seen and hated both me and my Father. 25 But this cometh to pass, that the word might be fulfilled that is written in their law, They hated me without a cause. 26 But when the Comforter is come, whom I will send unto you from the Father, even the Spirit of truth, which proceedeth from the Father, he shall testify of me: 27 and ye also shall bear witness, because ye have been with me from the beginning.

DEVOTION

The Power of Attorney

This is the last week and the fire turns up for this devotion! Jesus begins to tell Philip and the other disciples that He's leaving. However, if they believe on His name they will do greater works than even Jesus did! He actually says the words, "And whatsoever you ask in My name, that will I do that the Father may be glorified in the Son, if you ask anything in My name I will do it". He says it again in John 15:7, "If you abide in Me and My words abide in you, you shall ask what you want and it will be done". He says it AGAIN in John 15:16, "Whatever you ask of the Father in My name, He will give it to you". Don't you think that if Jesus said this three times in one conversation, that it must hold some extreme value to the believer? He keeps saying ask! And when you ask make sure to ask in His name.

A few years ago we had to sell our house to move to Atlanta to start a church. The house sold in two weeks, however, on the closing date of the sale of the house, we were not able to be there because we had already moved to Atlanta. I didn't know what to do! I found out that I could sign a paper called "Power of Attorney". If we could find somebody that we trusted to sign the closing papers, this power of attorney gave us the ability to have somebody act as us in our place, as if we were the ones signing. That's exactly what happened when Jesus put His blood on us. He kept telling the disciples you're going to ask anything "in My name" and it will happen as if I'm in the room!

The Scriptures also call us as believers, ambassadors. Meaning we carry out the functions of the kingdom of God here on earth, as it is in heaven. Sound familiar? Jesus taught His disciples to pray, thy kingdom come thy will be done ON EARTH, as it is in heaven.

The kingdom of God is established on the earth through the believer! You have the ability to ask IN THE NAME OF JESUS!!!!! Look what Peter and John did in Acts. They told the man at the gate Beautiful who had been lame for several years, "Silver and gold have I none, but such as I have, I give to you! IN THE NAME OF JESUS get up".

Mark 16:15 says these signs will follow those who believe...IN MY NAME...(go read it), believe it!

No one can talk you out of what God says is yours. Yes, heaven is His kingdom but He has given us the Power of Attorney to operate here on the earth with His name, JESUS!

What did the words of Jesus speak to you today?

_____
_____
_____
_____
_____

How can you apply them to your life?

_____
_____
_____
_____
_____

John 16

1 These things have I spoken unto you, that ye should not be offended. 2 They shall put you out of the synagogues: yea, the time cometh, that whosoever killeth you will think that he doeth God service. 3 And these things will they do unto you, because they have not known the Father, nor me. 4 But these things have I told you, that when the time shall come, ye may remember that I told you of them. And these things I said not unto you at the beginning, because I was with you. 5 But now I go my way to him that sent me; and none of you asketh me, Whither goest thou? 6 But because I have said these things unto you, sorrow hath filled your heart. 7 Nevertheless I tell you the truth; It is expedient for you that I go away: for if I go not away, the Comforter will not come unto you; but if I depart, I will send him unto you. 8 And when he is come, he will reprove the world of sin, and of righteousness, and of judgment: 9 of sin, because they believe not on me; 10 of righteousness, because I go to my Father, and ye see me no more; 11 of judgment, because the prince of this world is judged. 12 I have yet many things to say unto you, but ye cannot bear them now. 13 Howbeit when he, the Spirit of truth, is come, he will guide you into all truth: for he shall not speak of himself; but whatsoever he shall hear, that shall he speak: and he will shew you things to come. 14 He shall glorify me: for he shall receive of mine, and shall shew it unto you. 15 All things that the Father hath are mine: therefore said I, that he shall take of mine, and shall shew it unto you. 16 A little while, and ye shall not see me: and again, a little while, and ye shall see me, because I go to the Father.

To his disciples

19 Do ye inquire among yourselves of that I said, A little while, and ye shall not see me: and again, a little while, and ye shall see me? 20 Verily, verily, I say unto you, that ye shall weep and lament, but the world shall rejoice: and ye shall be sorrowful, but your sorrow shall be turned into joy. 21 A woman when she is in travail hath sorrow, because her hour is come: but as soon as she is delivered of the child, she remembereth no more the anguish, for joy that a man is born into the world. 22 And ye now therefore have sorrow: but I will see you again, and your heart shall rejoice, and your joy no man taketh from you. 23 And in that day ye shall ask me nothing. Verily, verily, I say unto you, Whatsoever ye shall ask the Father in my name, he will give it you. 24 Hitherto have ye asked nothing in my name: ask, and ye shall receive, that your joy may be full. 25 These things have I spoken unto you in proverbs: but the time cometh, when I shall no more speak unto you in proverbs, but I shall shew you plainly of the Father. 26 At that day ye shall ask in my name: and I say not unto you, that I will pray the Father for you: 27 for the Father himself loveth you, because ye have loved me, and have believed that I came out from God. 28 I came forth from the Father, and am come into the world: again, I leave the world, and go to the Father. 31 Do ye now believe? 32 Behold, the hour cometh, yea, is now come, that ye shall be scattered, every man to his own, and shall leave me alone: and yet I am not alone, because the Father is with me. 33 These things I have spoken unto you, that in me ye might have peace. In the world ye shall have tribulation: but be of good cheer; I have overcome the world.

John 17
Praying

1 Father, the hour is come; glorify thy Son, that thy Son also may glorify thee: 2 as thou hast given him power over all flesh, that he should give eternal life to as many as thou hast given him. 3 And this is life eternal, that they might know thee the only true God, and Jesus Christ, whom thou hast sent. 4 I have glorified thee on the earth: I have finished the work which thou gavest me to do. 5 And now, O Father, glorify thou me with thine own self with the glory which I had with thee before the world was. 6 I have manifested thy name unto the men which thou gavest me out of the world: thine they were, and thou gavest them me; and they have kept thy word. 7 Now they have known that all things whatsoever thou hast given me are of thee. 8 For I have given unto them the words which thou gavest me; and they have received them, and have known surely that I came out from thee, and they have believed that thou didst send me. 9 I pray for them: I pray not for the world, but for them which thou hast given me; for they are thine. 10 And all mine are thine, and thine are mine; and I am glorified in them. 11 And now I am no more in the world, but these are in the world, and I come to thee. Holy Father, keep through thine own name those whom thou hast given me, that they may be one, as we are. 12 While I was with them in the world, I kept them in thy name: those that thou gavest me I have kept, and none of them is lost, but the son of perdition; that the scripture might be fulfilled. 13 And now come I to thee; and these things I speak in the world, that they might have my joy fulfilled in themselves.

14 I have given them thy word; and the world hath hated them, because they are not of the world, even as I am not of the world. 15 I pray not that thou shouldest take them out of the world, but that thou shouldest keep them from the evil.

16 They are not of the world, even as I am not of the world.

17 Sanctify them through thy truth: thy word is truth.

18 As thou hast sent me into the world, even so have I also sent them into the world. 19 And for their sakes I sanctify myself, that they also might be sanctified through the truth. 20 Neither pray I for these alone, but for them also which shall believe on me through their word; 21 that they all may be one; as thou, Father, art in me, and I in thee, that they also may be one in us: that the world may believe that thou hast sent me. 22 And the glory which thou gavest me I have given them; that they may be one, even as we are one: 23 I in them, and thou in me, that they may be made perfect in one; and that the world may know that thou hast sent me, and hast loved them, as thou hast loved me. 24 Father, I will that they also, whom thou hast given me, be with me where I am; that they may behold my glory, which thou hast given me: for thou lovedst me before the foundation of the world. 25 O righteous Father, the world hath not known thee: but I have known thee, and these have known that thou hast sent me. 26 And I have declared unto them thy name, and will declare it: that the love wherewith thou hast loved me may be in them, and I in them.

DEVOTION

He's Coming for You!

John 16 is pretty much the job description of the Holy Spirit. Jesus is telling the disciples what the Holy Spirit will do through them and everyone, if they believe. The Holy Spirit is not an "it", rather a person, "He". An actual person operating through the believer! HE will comfort. HE will tell you. HE will reprove the world of sin. HE will guide you. HE will not speak of Himself but whatever He hears, HE will speak. HE shall glorify Jesus. HE will tell you of things to come. HE will take what is Mine and show it to you.

Jesus said, "It is expedient that I leave because if I don't go HE will not come to you". According to the Bible, when somebody receives Jesus as their Lord and Savior, the Holy Spirit comes into their lives. However, the baptism of the Holy Spirit, that we read of in Acts, is subsequent to the "infilling" at salvation. When Jesus was about to be transformed at the end of His time on earth, He breathed upon the disciples and they received the Holy Spirit. However, they had not operated in the gifts nor the power and authority that He would bring to their lives. PLEASE MAKE SURE YOUR LIFE AS A BELIEVER IS LIVED FULLY!

There are three levels of the Holy Spirit in your life:
1. Around you
2. Upon you
3. Within you

"Around you" is when you are in close proximity of somebody that the Holy Spirit is using. Typically, when you are living in sin and step into the close proximity of someone filled with the Holy Spirit, you will feel conviction. You will feel something without anybody saying anything. Condemnation comes from without...somebody speaking negatively about you. Conviction however, comes from within...an inward feeling of something needing to change in my life.

"Upon you" is when you are being changed by the glory of the Lord through the Holy Spirit. Many times you would see this in the Old Testament as it would say, "The Holy Spirit came upon...". People like Saul would prophesy, Elijah would do a mighty act and so on.

"Within you" is a completely different category! This is the Holy Spirit working within you. He is baptizing you with fire and purging out things in you! He also is operating within you. Think about most people who walk in space. They are out there in these things called spacesuits. However, the spacesuit is only doing what the man inside is telling it to do. That's the same description of what the Holy Spirit does through us! When we are completely yielded to Him, He begins to operate through us and only does the things that He sees and hears from heaven. He only agrees with God. He cannot agree with fear or doubt. This is why it's important that we pray prayers of faith and prayers that are rooted in the word of God. That is the only thing the Holy Spirit agrees with.

Today, pray prayers of faith and agree with the Spirit of God operating on the inside of you. If you want to know what He believes, read this book again and again and claim everything Jesus did that you also can do through that name!!

What did the words of Jesus speak to you today?

_____
_____
_____
_____
_____

How can you apply them to your life?

_____
_____
_____
_____
_____

John 18

In a garden over the brook Cedron, to Judas, a band of men, and officers from the chief priests and Pharisees

4 Whom seek ye? 5 I am he. 7 Whom seek ye? 8 I have told you that I am he: if therefore ye seek me, let these go their way:

To Peter

11 Put up thy sword into the sheath: the cup which my Father hath given me, shall I not drink it?

In the palace of the high priest, to Caiaphas

20 I spake openly to the world; I ever taught in the synagogue, and in the temple, whither the Jews always resort; and in secret have I said nothing. 21 Why askest thou me? Ask them which heard me, what I have said unto them: behold, they know what I said.

To one of the officers

23 If I have spoken evil, bear witness of the evil: but if well, why smitest thou me?

In the judgment hall, to Pilate, when asked, "Art thou the King of the Jews?"

34 Sayest thou this thing of thyself, or did others tell it thee of me? 36 My kingdom is not of this world: if my kingdom were of this world, then would my servants fight, that I should not be delivered to the Jews: but now is my kingdom not from hence. 37 Thou sayest that I am a king. To this end was I born, and for this cause came I into the world, that I should bear witness unto the truth. Every one that is of the truth heareth my voice.

In the judgment hall, to Pilate
John 19

11 Thou couldest have no power at all against me, except it were given thee from above: therefore he that delivered me unto thee hath the greater sin.

On the cross, to his mother

26 Woman, behold thy son!

To the disciple whom he loved

27 Behold thy mother!

On the cross

28 I thirst. 30 It is finished:

Without, at the sepulchre, to Mary Magdalene
John 20

15 Woman, why weepest thou? Whom seekest thou?
16 Mary.

17 Touch me not; for I am not yet ascended to my Father: but go to my brethren, and say unto them, I ascend unto my Father, and your Father; and to my God, and your God.
In the midst of the disciples behind closed doors 19 Peace be unto you. 21 Peace be unto you: as my Father hath sent me, even so send I you. 22 Receive ye the Holy Ghost: 23 whose soever sins ye remit, they are remitted unto them; and whose soever sins ye retain, they are retained.
Eight days later 26 Peace be unto you.

To Thomas
27 Reach hither thy finger, and behold my hands; and reach hither thy hand, and thrust it into my side: and be not faithless, but believing. 29Thomas, because thou hast seen me, thou hast believed: blessed are they that have not seen, and yet have believed.

John 21
On the shore of the sea of Tiberias, to the disciples
5 Children, have ye any meat? 6 Cast the net on the right side of the ship, and ye shall find. 10 Bring of the fish which ye have now caught. 12 Come and dine.

To Simon Peter
15 Simon, son of Jonas, lovest thou me more than these? Feed my lambs. 16 Simon, son of Jonas, lovest thou me? Feed my sheep. 17 Simon, son of Jonas, lovest thou me? Feed my sheep. 18 Verily, verily, I say unto thee, When thou wast young, thou girdedst thyself, and walkedst whither thou wouldest: but when thou shalt be old, thou shalt stretch forth thy hands, and another shall gird thee, and carry thee whither thou wouldest not. 19 Follow me.
Answering Peter's question, concerning the disciple who wrote these things: we know that his testimony is true, "Lord, and what shall this man do?" 22 If I will that he tarry till I come, what is that to thee? follow thou me.

DEVOTION

Seeing Without Eyes!

Jesus presents Himself to Thomas in John 20:27. Thomas says, "If I don't see Him, I won't believe". It wasn't enough for Thomas to hear about Jesus resurrecting, he had to see with his own eyes. Jesus tells Thomas, "Be not faithless, but believe". He goes on to tell him, "Blessed are those who have not seen and yet believe".

People often say they know that they're going to heaven. The question back to them that we say is, "How do you know?". You see, no one gives you a piece of paper saying you have a ticket, or a pass. Romans 10:9 says that when we confess with our mouths and believe in our hearts that Jesus is our Lord, we are saved. OUR FAITH TO RECEIVE SALVATION IS FROM OUR MOUTH and HEART...NOT OUR EYES!

Jesus calls everyone that has not seen Him, but yet believes, blessed! Faith in it's true definition is the substance of things hoped for and the evidence of things NOT SEEN! Our faith in Jesus has to go farther than just seeing Him with our physical eyes. We must see Him in our hearts. Can you believe when you cannot see Him? Obviously, when you receive salvation, the same faith that gave you an entrance into heaven is the same faith you should use when all hell is breaking loose in your life and you can't understand why. ONLY BELIEVE! It is the key to everything in your life! BELIEVE! See Jesus working in your life, first in your heart! That's faith! Faith has the ability to change our world when we envision it in our hearts!

What did the words of Jesus speak to you today?

_____

_____

_____

_____

_____

How can you apply them to your life?

_____

_____

_____

_____

_____

Acts

Chapter 1

4 And, being assembled together with them, commanded them that they should not depart from Jerusalem, but wait for the promise of the Father, which, saith he, ye have heard of me. 5 For John truly baptized with water; but ye shall be baptized with the Holy Ghost not many days hence. 6 When they therefore were come together, they asked of him, saying, Lord, wilt thou at this time restore again the kingdom to Israel? 7 And he said unto them, It is not for you to know the times or the seasons, which the Father hath put in his own power. 8 But ye shall receive power, after that the Holy Ghost is come upon you: and ye shall be witnesses unto me both in Jerusalem, and in all Judaea, and in Samaria, and unto the uttermost part of the earth.

Chapter 9

1 And Saul, yet breathing out threatenings and slaughter against the disciples of the Lord, went unto the high priest, 2 And desired of him letters to Damascus to the synagogues, that if he found any of this way, whether they were men or women, he might bring them bound unto Jerusalem. 3 And as he journeyed, he came near Damascus: and suddenly there shined round about him a light from heaven: 4 And he fell to the earth, and heard a voice saying unto him, Saul, Saul, why persecutest thou me? 5 And he said, Who art thou, Lord? And the Lord said, I am Jesus whom thou persecutest: it is hard for thee to kick against the pricks. 6 And he trembling and astonished said, Lord, what wilt thou have me to do? And the Lord said unto him, Arise, and go into the city, and it shall be told thee what thou must do. 7 And the men which journeyed with him stood speechless, hearing a voice, but seeing no man. 8 And Saul arose from the earth; and when his eyes were opened, he saw no man: but they led him by the hand, and brought him into Damascus. 9 And he was three days without sight, and neither did eat nor drink. 10 And there was a certain disciple at Damascus, named Ananias; and to him said the Lord in a vision, Ananias. And he said, Behold, I am here, Lord. 11 And the Lord said unto him, Arise, and go into the street which is called Straight, and inquire in the house of Judas for one called Saul, of Tarsus: for, behold, he prayeth, 12 And hath seen in a vision a man named Ananias coming in, and putting his hand on him, that he might receive his sight. 13 Then Ananias answered, Lord, I have heard by many of this man, how much evil he hath done to thy saints at Jerusalem: 14 And here he hath authority from the chief priests to bind all that call on thy name. 15 But the Lord said unto him, Go thy way: for he is a chosen vessel unto me, to bear my name before the Gentiles, and kings, and the children of Israel: 16 For I will shew him how great things he must suffer for my name's sake. 17 And Ananias went his way, and entered into the house; and putting his hands on him said, Brother Saul, the Lord, even Jesus, that appeared unto thee in the way as thou camest, hath sent me, that thou mightest receive thy sight, and be filled with the Holy Ghost. 18 And immediately there fell from his eyes as it had been scales: and he received sight forthwith, and arose, and was baptized.

DEVOTION

The Baptism of FIRE

Even though the gospels, Matthew, Mark, Luke and John are where the stories of Jesus are mainly, there are also moments in Acts and Revelation where He speaks as well.

Jesus speaks in Acts chapter 1, "You shall receive POWER". The word power is *dunamis* in the Greek and where we get the word DYNAMITE...EXPLOSIVE! Jesus tells them that they are going to receive something so powerful that the whole world will change! The baptism of the Holy Spirit will come upon them. They would be filled with what Jesus was filled with! This did not stop at Acts! The Bible says that as many as the Lord calls, receive this baptism!

On that first Pentecost Sunday in the New Testament, 120 people were praying in one accord and in one place and a sound from heaven, of a rushing, mighty wind came in and filled the house! Divided tongues of fire set upon each one of them and they were filled with the Holy Spirit and began to speak and other tongues. Each one received a tongue of fire! Each one of us can receive our own baptism of fire power!

The baptism of the Holy Spirit inside of each one of us purges and cleanses like a refiner. Psalm 66:10 says that our God has tested us and refined us as silver is refined. That baptism of fire that we get when we are baptized in the Holy Spirit purifies us! The silversmith heats up the furnace and puts the silver in. The fire brings to the surface all impurities that are in the silver. The silversmith then takes away the mixture of dross that was in the silver. The fire is what revealed the impurities! Do you know when the silversmith knows that the silver has been refined? When he can look in the silver and see his image, he knows that the silver is purified.

When you pray for the baptism of the Holy Spirit, He also comes with a purification working on the inside of the believer. The Holy Spirit works inside of you to draw out of you everything that is not of God. We are earthen vessels housing a treasure! When the Holy Spirit comes on the inside of you every fruit of the Spirit begins to operate and the gifts of the Spirit are accessible to EACH BELIEVER!

What did the words of Jesus speak to you today?

_____
_____
_____
_____
_____

How can you apply them to your life?

_____
_____
_____
_____
_____

Revelation
Chapter 1

8 I am Alpha and Omega, the beginning and the ending, which is, and which was, and which is to come, the Almighty. 11 I am Alpha and Omega, the first and the last: and, What thou seest, write in a book, and send it unto the seven churches which are in Asia; unto Ephesus, and unto Smyrna, and unto Pergamos, and unto Thyatira, and unto Sardis, and unto Philadelphia, and unto Laodicea. 17 Fear not; I am the first and the last: 18 I am he that liveth, and was dead; and, behold, I am alive for evermore, Amen; and have the keys of hell and of death. 19 Write the things which thou hast seen, and the things which are, and the things which shall be hereafter; 20 the mystery of the seven stars which thou sawest in my right hand, and the seven golden candlesticks. The seven stars are the angels of the seven churches: and the seven candlesticks which thou sawest are the seven churches.

Chapter 2

1 Unto the angel of the church of Ephesus write; These things saith he that holdeth the seven stars in his right hand, who walketh in the midst of the seven golden candlesticks; 2 I know thy works, and thy labour, and thy patience, and how thou canst not bear them which are evil: and thou hast tried them which say they are apostles, and are not, and hast found them liars: 3 and hast borne, and hast patience, and for my name's sake hast laboured, and hast not fainted.
4 Nevertheless I have somewhat against thee, because thou hast left thy first love. 5 Remember therefore from whence thou art fallen, and repent, and do the first works; or else I will come unto thee quickly, and will remove thy candlestick out of his place, except thou repent. 6 But this thou hast, that thou hatest the deeds of the Nicolaitans, which I also hate. 7 He that hath an ear, let him hear what the Spirit saith unto the churches; To him that overcometh will I give to eat of the tree of life, which is in the midst of the paradise of God.

DEVOTION

Don't Lose Your First Love...The Cross is Vertical and Horizontal

Jesus comes on the scene in Revelation declaring who He is! "I am the ALPHA, OMEGA, the FIRST and LAST! I'm the one that started this thing and I'm the one that will finish it! There's no reason to fear, I hold the keys!" Man, what an incredible beginning to this book. If you ever wonder who is in charge of everything going on, remember Jesus is in complete control and nothing is out of His dominion.

He writes to the church of Ephesus and says you all have left your first love. He says, "I see your labor, I see that you see the error in people and it is legitimate. However, I have this AGAINST you. Go back to that which you loved first".

Isn't it amazing that we fall in love with Jesus so strongly at the beginning of our relationship with Him and we want to be just like Him? Then we realize again that even though we are saved, we are still living in a world full of people that are not! And more aggravating than that is when people act saved on Sunday and are not the other 6 days!!

We can sometimes become bitter, even as church folk, as we do the will of God in our lives but at the same time have anger and resentment towards others. Matthew 22:37 reminds us of what Jesus says is the most important thing for the believer. "You shall love the Lord your God with all your heart, soul, and mind and then the second you shall love your neighbor as yourself."

Jesus told a man, "If you don't stop being so bitter about people working out their salvation, I'm going to remove your influence and your candlestick. In other words, other people's actions should not dictate yours. If you live long enough as a Christian, you're going to realize that some people are not in this thing for the right reasons, but that should never change you and the love you have for God and God's people.

THE CROSS HAS TWO DIRECTIONS - vertical and horizontal. You cannot have a vertical relationship with God and eliminate a horizontal relationship with God's people. I would even go on to say that your relationship with God is no stronger than your relationship with God's people. Jesus said you will know them by their love for one another. Love is eternal! It's the greatest of faith, hope, and love! You can't have faith only and hope only and forget the LOVE. The nails didn't hold Him to His cross, His love for us did! He even said during His crucifixion, "Father, forgive them for they know not what they do". AMAZING GRACE! We must share that amazing grace with others as well!

What did the words of Jesus speak to you today?

_____

_____

_____

_____

_____

How can you apply them to your life?

_____

_____

_____

_____

_____

Chapter 2

8 And unto the angel of the church in Smyrna write; These things saith the first and the last, which was dead, and is alive; 9 I know thy works, and tribulation, and poverty, (but thou art rich) and I know the blasphemy of them which say they are Jews, and are not, but are the synagogue of Satan. 10 Fear none of those things which thou shalt suffer: behold, the devil shall cast some of you into prison, that ye may be tried; and ye shall have tribulation ten days: be thou faithful unto death, and I will give thee a crown of life. 11 He that hath an ear, let him hear what the Spirit saith unto the churches; He that overcometh shall not be hurt of the second death. 12 And to the angel of the church in Pergamos write; These things saith he which hath the sharp sword with two edges; 13 I know thy works, and where thou dwellest, even where Satan's seat is: and thou holdest fast my name, and hast not denied my faith, even in those days wherein Antipas was my faithful martyr, who was slain among you, where Satan dwelleth. 14 But I have a few things against thee, because thou hast there them that hold the doctrine of Balaam, who taught Balac to cast a stumblingblock before the children of Israel, to eat things sacrificed unto idols, and to commit fornication. 15 So hast thou also them that hold the doctrine of the Nicolaitans, which thing I hate. 16 Repent; or else I will come unto thee quickly, and will fight against them with the sword of my mouth. 17 He that hath an ear, let him hear what the Spirit saith unto the churches; To him that overcometh will I give to eat of the hidden manna, and will give him a white stone, and in the stone a new name written, which no man knoweth saving he that receiveth it.

18 And unto the angel of the church in Thyatira write; These things saith the Son of God, who hath his eyes like unto a flame of fire, and his feet are like fine brass; 19 I know thy works, and charity, and service, and faith, and thy patience, and thy works; and the last to be more than the first. 20 Notwithstanding I have a few things against thee, because thou sufferest that woman Jezebel, which calleth herself a prophetess, to teach and to seduce my servants to commit fornication, and to eat things sacrificed unto idols. 21 And I gave her space to repent of her fornication; and she repented not. 22 Behold, I will cast her into a bed, and them that commit adultery with her into great tribulation, except they repent of their deeds. 23 And I will kill her children with death; and all the churches shall know that I am he which searcheth the reins and hearts: and I will give unto every one of you according to your works. 24 But unto you I say, and unto the rest in Thyatira, as many as have not this doctrine, and which have not known the depths of Satan, as they speak; I will put upon you none other burden. 25 But that which ye have already hold fast till I come. 26 And he that overcometh, and keepeth my works unto the end, to him will I give power over the nations: 27 and he shall rule them with a rod of iron; as the vessels of a potter shall they be broken to shivers: even as I received of my Father. 28 And I will give him the morning star. 29 He that hath an ear, let him hear what the Spirit saith unto the churches.

DEVOTION

Rated R Churches
Persecuted, Corrupt and Compromising Churches...

Jesus speaks to three churches in this daily devotion. The first one is being heavily persecuted and He encourages those to stay faithful. The second church is compromising and is committing sexual immoralities. Jesus says, "You're dwelling where Satan's throne is". WOW! Jesus is talking to church folk!!

It's one thing to commit a sin but it's an entirely different thing to continue in it in the name of Jesus. Jesus didn't die on Good Friday so that we could have fun on Fat Tuesday. He wasn't sinless so that we can stay sinful and lush in our pleasures and flesh while singing away in Zion. No! We don't get to do whatever we want to do. If we truly have the love of Jesus in us, we don't WANT to do the things that happen around Satan's throne. We are forged as a new creation to conform to His image.

These churches that are compromising and corrupt are RATED R CHURCHES. Seems like today we have that same thought running rampant in our churches. It's okay to watch whatever you want to, listen to whatever you want to, go to the concerts where they blaspheme God's name repeatedly and do sexual acts on stages, in the name of entertainment. Yet we can still sing on Sunday and sin on Monday and God has enough grace for us to slip on into heaven. We live in a "50 shades of gray" generation. We need to be in a 50 Shades of Red church!! Many say these are just personal convictions but I'm reading my Bible where Jesus says, "I hate them" and "Immoralities are where Satan dwells". He also goes on to say these are stumbling blocks for your children. Your kids will grow up thinking watching sex on a screen in the movie theater and going to church is okay! They will think praising well-known artists that say GodD#*mn and twerk and gyrate on stage and going to church is okay. They will raise up and have low or no standards and call it grace! God forbid!

Today let the Holy Spirit convict your heart if you're involved in anything that is not the nature of Christ. Father cleanse me! Take this sin from my heart. This immorality and this greed and lust for more of the world! CHANGE ME!

What did the words of Jesus speak to you today?

_____

_____

_____

_____

_____

How can you apply them to your life?

_____

_____

_____

_____

_____

Chapter 3

1 And unto the angel of the church in Sardis write; These things saith he that hath the seven Spirits of God, and the seven stars; I know thy works, that thou hast a name that thou livest, and art dead. 2 Be watchful, and strengthen the things which remain, that are ready to die: for I have not found thy works perfect before God. 3Remember therefore how thou hast received and heard, and hold fast, and repent. If therefore thou shalt not watch, I will come on thee as a thief, and thou shalt not know what hour I will come upon thee. 4 Thou hast a few names even in Sardis which have not defiled their garments; and they shall walk with me in white: for they are worthy. 5 He that overcometh, the same shall be clothed in white raiment; and I will not blot out his name out of the book of life, but I will confess his name before my Father, and before his angels. 6 He that hath an ear, let him hear what the Spirit saith unto the churches. 7 And to the angel of the church in Philadelphia write; These things saith he that is holy, he that is true, he that hath the key of David, he that openeth, and no man shutteth; and shutteth, and no man openeth;

8 I know thy works: behold, I have set before thee an open door, and no man can shut it: for thou hast a little strength, and hast kept my word, and hast not denied my name.

9 Behold, I will make them of the synagogue of Satan, which say they are Jews, and are not, but do lie; behold, I will make them to come and worship before thy feet, and to know that I have loved thee. 10 Because thou hast kept the word of my patience, I also will keep thee from the hour of temptation, which shall come upon all the world, to try them that dwell upon the earth. 11 Behold, I come quickly: hold that fast which thou hast, that no man take thy crown.

12 Him that overcometh will I make a pillar in the temple of my God, and he shall go no more out: and I will write upon him the name of my God, and the name of the city of my God, which is new Jerusalem, which cometh down out of heaven from my God: and I will write upon him my new name. 13 He that hath an ear, let him hear what the Spirit saith unto the churches. 14 And unto the angel of the church of the Laodiceans write; These things saith the Amen, the faithful and true witness, the beginning of the creation of God; 15 I know thy works, that thou art neither cold nor hot: I would thou wert cold or hot. 16 So then because thou art lukewarm, and neither cold nor hot, I will spue thee out of my mouth. 17 Because thou sayest, I am rich, and increased with goods, and have need of nothing; and knowest not that thou art wretched, and miserable, and poor, and blind, and naked: 18 I counsel thee to buy of me gold tried in the fire, that thou mayest be rich; and white raiment, that thou mayest be clothed, and that the shame of thy nakedness do not appear; and anoint thine eyes with eye-salve, that thou mayest see. 19 As many as I love, I rebuke and chasten: be zealous therefore, and repent.

20 Behold, I stand at the door, and knock: if any man hear my voice, and open the door, I will come in to him, and will sup with him, and he with me. 21 To him that overcometh will I grant to sit with me in my throne, even as I also overcame, and am set down with my Father in his throne.

22 He that hath an ear, let him hear what the Spirit saith unto the churches.

DEVOTION

Lukewarm Church

This is getting heavy...two days out! Jesus is speaking to all of these churches about what needs to change! Today let's focus on the Laodicean church.

He told them they are unusable. They want both the world and God. In Laodicea, there were three streams. There was a hot stream, a cold stream and a lukewarm stream that would flow in the city.

This church knew exactly what Jesus was saying because the hot and cold streams were able to be used for drinking, bathing, cooking and more. But there was a lukewarm stream that was contaminated. It could not be used for anything even though it looked like the other streams. It had a mixture inside that was deadly.

In that last day God is not going to ask us about our church attendance, our church size or budget. He's going to ask us about our effectiveness. Were we a house of prayer more than a house of preaching, or a house of singing? Did we want power or did we want prestige? Did we want fresh fire or were we comfortable with fake fire? Did we complete the kingdom or did we compete with people in the kingdom. The Bible says woe to those who are at ease in Zion. These people are happy and satisfied being complacent and lukewarm. These will judge someone getting happy in church while they sit and stare during worship. They will twerk and jerk for the world but won't raise a hand in church. Help us God! Remember, Jesus is talking to church folk.

Help us Lord to continue to be radical in our commitment to you. Help us to stay repenting, convicted, nonjudgmental and at the same time full of God. The Bible says in the last days perilous times will come. For people will have a form of godliness but they will deny the power. They're going to look like church but they aren't going to be the church. They're very lukewarm and are satisfied being status quo.

To those who are upholding the blood-stained banner we say to you, PREACH ON. You may not be popular, you may not be in the in crowd, but your audience will no doubt realize that you're not representing them, you're representing God. And in this season and generation, we need voices to declare for the people of God to walk with integrity.

What did the words of Jesus speak to you today?

_____

_____

_____

_____

_____

How can you apply them to your life?

_____

_____

_____

_____

_____

Chapter 16

15 Behold, I come as a thief. Blessed is he that watcheth, and keepeth his garments, lest he walk naked, and they see his shame. 17 Behold, I come quickly: blessed is he that keepeth the sayings of the prophecy of this book.

Chapter 21

6 It is done. I am Alpha and Omega, the beginning and the end. I will give unto him that is athirst of the fountain of the water of life freely. 7 He that overcometh shall inherit all things; and I will be his God, and he shall be my son.

Chapter 22

6 These sayings are faithful and true: and the Lord God of the holy prophets sent his angel to shew unto his servants the things which must shortly be done. 12 And, behold, I come quickly; and my reward is with me, to give every man according as his work shall be. 13 I am Alpha and Omega, the beginning and the end, the first and the last. 16 I Jesus have sent mine angel to testify unto you these things in the churches. I am the root and the offspring of David, and the bright and morning star. 17 And the Spirit and the bride say, Come. 20 He which testifieth these things saith, surely I come quickly.

DEVOTION

WIRED FOR LIFE!

This is it! This is the last day. You have spent 50 days reading the words of Jesus. Congratulations!

When somebody puts a letter together, they teach you in English to make sure you start the letter out with a line explaining what the body of the letter is going to say next. Then close it out with a recap and a takeaway of what this letter was all about. We see Jesus doing that in His last words of the Holy Bible. "Behold I come as a thief so keep watching, surely I come quickly!"

When He says keep watching, it also means keep occupying. Keep building the kingdom, keep your eyes on the truth and keep doing what God has called you to do. He says in this, every person will receive a reward according to his work.

Keep the fire on your coals burning! We encourage you to make a decision today to move forward with power and commitment. Don't be wishy-washy and don't do one thing and say another, but keep your hand fast on the plow, never looking back, working for the kingdom of God, loving people, bearing the fruit of the Spirit, being open to being used by the Holy Spirit every day. This is your new birth. This is what you were called to do, to be like Jesus and to be an ambassador for the kingdom of God. GO FORTH WIRED!

What did the words of Jesus speak to you today?

_____

_____

_____

_____

_____

How can you apply them to your life?

_____

_____

_____

_____

_____

Final Thoughts

Yes, believe it or not you have finished your 50 day journey. This is however not the end but a God given beginning.

No doubt your life has been changed as you have read and studied the Words of Jesus. Please review your responses at the end of each day's devotion and begin applying those things to your life.

You will continue to see a difference In your own life and the lives of those around you as you allow the Holy Spirit to enlighten and empower you to do everything He has spoken to you.